SCMC Account No.28

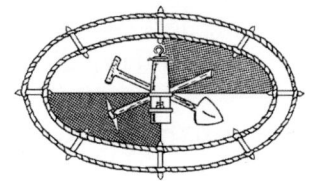

Aerial Ropeways of Shropshire

by

Michael Shaw, David Poyner & Robert Evans

ISBN: 978-0-9553019-5-7

© Copyright Michael Shaw, David Poyner, Robert Evans, Shropshire Caving & Mining Club 2015

Published by the Shropshire Caving and Mining Club

Details of other publications and videos available from the Club, membership details and other information related to the Shropshire Caving & Mining Club are on the Club website:

www.shropshirecmc.org.uk

Design and Layout: Kelvin Lake

The content of this Account are the opinion of the individual authors and not necessarily those of the Shropshire Caving & Mining Club

All images are reproduced from the individual authors collections unless otherwise stated.

The right of each named contributor to be identified as the author of their individual work(s) has been asserted by them in accordance with the Copyright, Designs and Patents Act 1988.

All rights reserved. No part of this publication may be reproduced, stored in a retrieval system or transmitted in any form or by any means without the prior written permission of the publisher.

All mines are potentially dangerous and should not be explored without an experienced guide. Permission should always be obtained before venturing on private property and the mention of a particular site does not imply any right of access.

Printed in Great Britain by Cambrian Printers, Aberystwyth

Contents

1. Introduction 1
   Ropeways in Shropshire 4

Part 1: East Shropshire

2. Catherton Ropeway 5
3. Bayton Ropeway 12
4. Billingsley Ropeway 17
5. Alveley Colliery Ropeway 24
6. Cosford Water Works 29
7. Minor Ropeways 34

Part 2: West Shropshire

The Stiperstones' Ropeways - Introduction 37
8. The Bog line and branches 38
   The Main Line 39
   The Perkins Beach Branch 47
   The Buxton Quarry Branch 48
9. Huglith line 50
10. Ropeway Staff 54
11. Fieldwork 55
    Bog Line Fieldwork 55
    The Bog Mine Aerial Ropeway Terminus 57
    Rope Stretch 59
    Huglith Line Fieldwork 61
    Perkins Beach Line Fieldwork 61
12. Imaginary Ropeways 62
13. Bibliography & Acknowledgements 63
Appendix A - Schedule of bases found during Fieldwork 64
    Bog Main Line 64
    Map 1 - Route of the Bog Ropeway 65
    Huglith Line 66
    Map 2 - Route of the Huglith Ropeway 67
    Perkins Beach Line 68
    Buxton Quarry Line 68
    Map 3 - Routes of the Perkins Beach and Buxton Quarry Lines 68

Robert Evans, FRICS, 1934-2014.

Robert Evans, a co-author of this book, died as the proofs were being prepared. Robert trained as a surveyor at Alveley Colliery and was an expert on the history of the Wyre Forest Coalfield.

DRP in particular wishes to acknowledge the immense contributions that Robert made to local mining history.

Above: Robert in recent years.

Below: Robert (on the right) working as a trainee surveyor at Alveley Colliery in 1953. Pat Ward, his linesman, is standing next to him.

(Aileen Evans)

1. Ropeways of Shropshire - Introduction

History

Simple ropeways have been used for centuries as a means of moving goods from one side of a gully or obstacle to another. In medieval manuscripts there are illustrations of inclined rope hoists and in 1608 the author Verantuis showed a diagram of passenger-carrying cable car, albeit one that was never built. The Dutch architect Adam Wybe used a ropeway to move earth across a moat for a building project in Danzig in 1644.[1] However, it was in Victorian times that ropeways were first widely adopted for transport, following the development of reliable wire ropes. The first practical system was patented in 1868 by Charles Hodgson, an Irish-born engineer living in Richmond in Surrey. This was a single-rope system where one rope both supported the buckets and was also used for hauling them (Figure 1.1). In 1869 Hodgson and a fellow engineer, William Carrington, formed the Wire Tramway Company and built two demonstration ropeways, one at gravel pit near Richmond and another at a Leicestershire granite quarry. The later was three miles long, connecting the quarry to the nearest railway and attracted considerable interest. In 1871 a two mile tramway which descended 2,000' was built according to Hodgson's designs at Treasure Hill in Nevada, USA. Also in the USA at the same time, Andrew Hallidie, a manufacturer of wire rope, developed his own system that had some significant advantages over Hodgson's design.[2] Hodgson and Carrington continued to refine their own designs; the Wire Rope Company was registered as a public company in 1871 and in 1872 a major ropeway was built in Antrim to reach a ironstone mine. The success of this can be judged that just a year later local carters destroyed it as it was threatening their livelihoods.

Figure 1.1: A typical ropeway bucket and clip.
(Ropeways as a means of transport, J. Pearce-Roe, Engineering Times, I, (1899), 308)

An alternative system was developed by Adolf Bleichert in Germany in 1872 involving two ropes. A static carrying rope bore the weight of the load and a moving haulage rope provided the propulsion. This allowed heavier weights to be carried. Bleichert began manufacturing in Leipzig in 1874 with Theodor Otto.[3] The double rope system became the method of choice on ropeways that carried heavy traffic, although the single rope system continued to exist alongside it. Indeed single rope systems underwent something of a revival at the start of the 20th century with improvements both in wire rope construction and also the introduction of balance beams with multiple sheaves to carry the rope on the pylons that supported it.[4]

Simple rope hoists were also developing on parallel lines to the ropeways of Hodgson, Carrington and Bleichert. Around 1860 in quarries in Pennsylvania, "Blondins" first appeared.[5] A "Blondin" was essentially a block and pulley that moved along a wire rope. It allowed large blocks of stone to be lifted off the ground and moved along the rope from the quarry face to the dressing floor. These devices were named after Charles Blondin, a Frenchman who walked over the Niagra Falls on a tightrope in 1859. In 1872 John Fyfe installed the first Blondin in Britain in his granite quarry near Aberdeen.[6] The firm of John M. Henderson of Aberdeen became heavily involved in ropeway installation in quarries and elsewhere from 1873.

Aerial ropeways had certain advantages over railways and tramroads. They could be used across terrain that was too steep or rugged for a railway. They were cheap to construct as they did not require a continuous length of track. For the same reason, they were also sometimes more acceptable to landowners as they resulted in minimal disturbance to the ground. However, they also had some important disadvantages. They were frequently associated with high running costs and were prone to breakdowns if not carefully maintained. In the mountainous parts of the USA or continental Europe, they found ready acceptance as railways were impractical. In the UK, this was far from the case. In 1906 when Henderson's built a ropeway for the construction of a dam across Loch Linnie in the West Highlands it was reported that no other form of transport could have been used to bring materials to the site. There were few other parts of the country where this could truthfully be said; most engineers preferred light railways with rope-worked inclines. None-the-less, by the end of the 19th Century it was clear that they could be useful solutions to some transport problems. The early 20th Century was the hay-day for British aerial ropeways as they complemented the miles of light railways on industrial sites throughout the country. Improvements in road transport and conveyors eventually rendered them superfluous. Although much favoured by the National Coal Board in the 1950s and 1960s, other users were abandoning them. With the contraction of coal mining and indeed most other extractive industries, they eventually became virtually extinct. One, at a brickworks at Claughton near Lancaster still runs at the time of writing but is due for replacement using ski lift technology.

Operation

In both the single and double cable systems the buckets were attached, via a cradle, to the rope(s) by a clip (Figure 1.1). There were numerous different designs of clips, all of which were claimed to grip the rope tightly and stop the buckets slipping. The buckets themselves were usually emptied manually by simple tipping. At either end of the ropeway would be the loading and discharge stations (Figures 1.2, 1.3). At these the buckets would be unclipped from the rope(s); the clips were usually designed so that this happened automatically. The endless carrying rope would pass round a return wheel. The buckets would run on a shunt rail; typically a long, U-shaped girder. The cradle, as well as carrying a clip to attach to the rope, would also have one or more wheels which would run on the shunt rail. In a two rope system, the wheels would also run on the carrying rope. Once on the shunt rail, the buckets could be moved by hand to be filled and unfilled. It was also possible to devise systems of points so that buckets could be moved from one shunt rail to another, effectively allowing them to be stored in sidings.

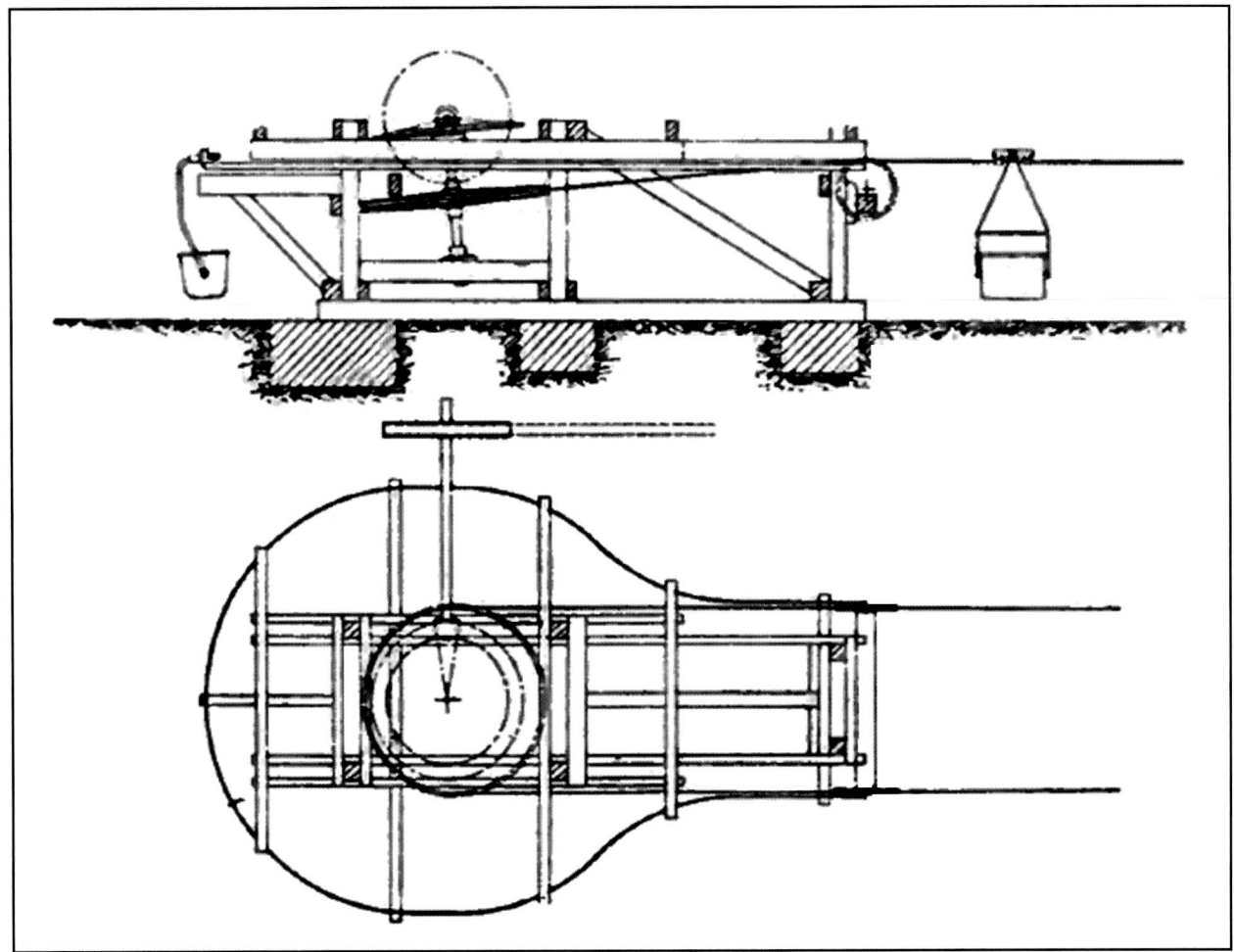

Figure 1.2: The driving station of a typical aerial ropeway. A belt drive transmits the power to the ropeway via the inclined spur wheel. The buckets move on a rail to take them clear of the drive mechanism.
(Ropeways as a means of transport, J. Pearce-Roe, Engineering Times, I, (1899), 305)

Although some ropeways ran in a straight line, on longer systems it was often necessary to go round a bend. This was normally achieved by an angle station. At this, the buckets would be detached from the rope and guided around the bend on curved shunt rails. The ropes were deflected by guide wheels. Normally the stations were designed so that the buckets would have enough momentum to pass round the rails unaided and automatically reattach themselves to the ropes. However, one or two workmen were often employed at the earlier angle stations to ensure the process worked properly.

In principle, where a ropeway transferred material downhill, it should have been self-acting with the weight of the full buckets descending enough to move the empty buckets back up. Although many ropeways were built at a favourable gradient, the vast majority were powered. This reflected the fact that many ropeways carried significant loads in both directions. The drive was usually transmitted to the return wheel at the loading station; power was normally either by steam engine or, latterly, electric motor. To keep the tension in the rope, one of the return wheels (usually at the discharge station) was mounted on a frame so that it could be moved. Wire ropes would stretch with use and so the return wheel would have to be gradually moved back down its frame. Normally the wheel was attached to a set of weights so that tensioning was done automatically. Once the wheel reached the limit of its travel, a section would need to be cut out of the rope and the two ends spliced together again so that it was shortened. The rope would have to be replaced every few years. With double rope systems the drive was typically applied through pulleys that were distinct from the return wheel; in these systems the tension was applied at the driving station (Figure 1.3).

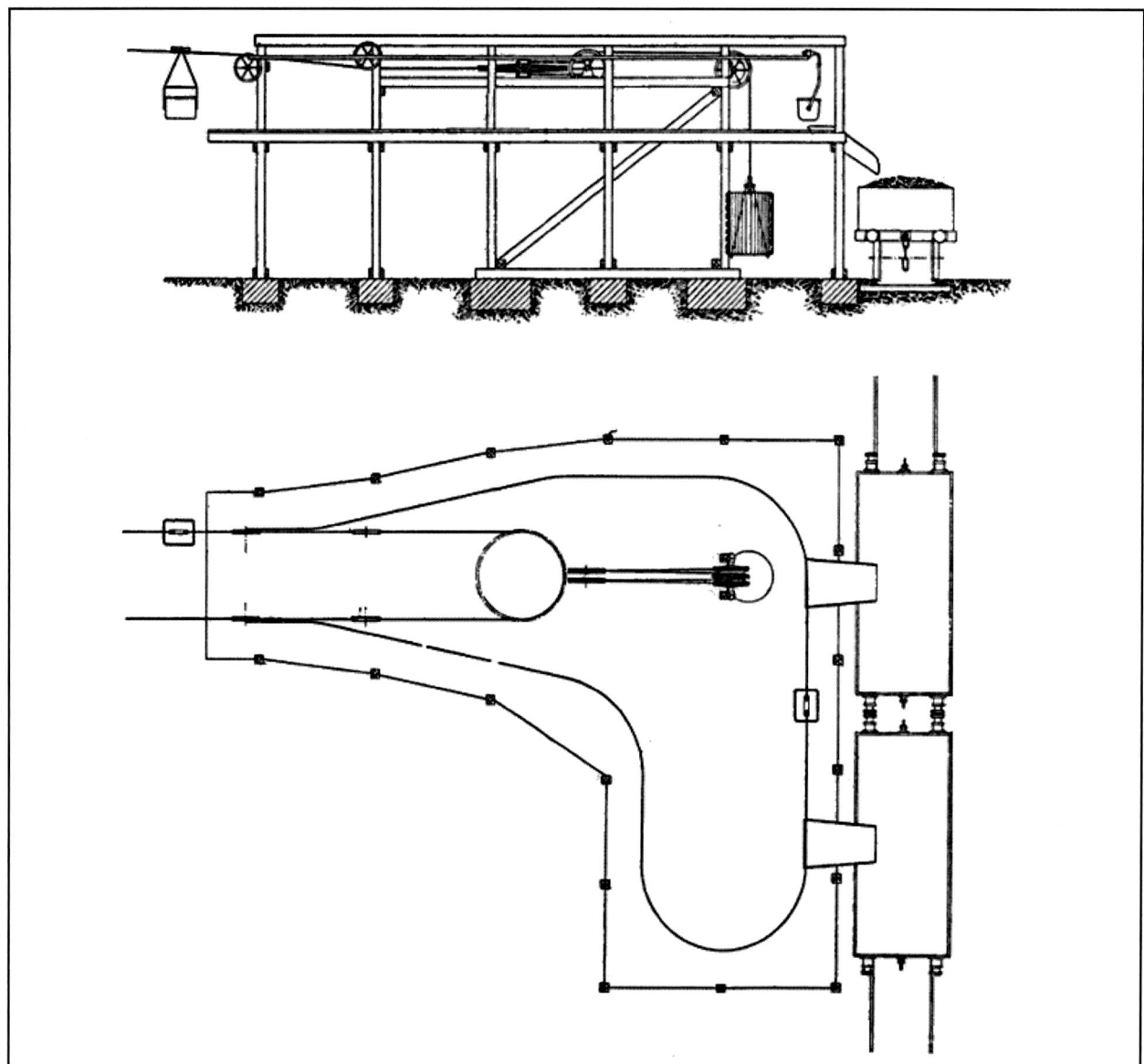

Figure 1.3: A ropeway terminus. The rope runs around the wheel whilst the buckets pass onto the U-shaped shunt rail. The return wheel is mounted on brackets in a frame and attached to weights, to keep the rope under tension. *(Ropeways as a means of transport, J. Pearce-Roe, Engineering Times, I, (1899), 306)*

Ropeways in Shropshire

Shropshire was not a pioneer in the use of aerial ropeways. By the time of Hodgson's patents, the most industrialised part of the county, the Coalbrookdale Coalfield, already had a highly developed transport system, largely based on tramways. Elsewhere, there was a good system of railways and these could readily be linked up with remote industrial sites by tramways and inclines. Thus there was little advantage in adopting the new technology. In 1901, the mining engineer Arthur C. Auden reported on the options to link a new quarry on top of the Brown Clee with the proposed Cleobury Mortimer and Ditton Priors Light Railway. In spite of the quarry being 1½ miles from the railhead and 1,000' higher, he recommended a rail-link via a rope-worked incline rather than an aerial ropeway. This was on account of what he felt would be the high operating costs of a ropeway and its poor reliability.[7] In this respect, Shropshire was typical of much of the rest of the country. Significant systems were not built until the years before the First World War and, apart from that at Cosford, were confined to just two parts of the county. In the south-east, ropeways around the Clee Hills and the Wyre Forest Coalfield were used for moving coal and stone. In the south-west, they were used for transport of barytes from the mines of the Stipperstones. Ultimately it seems that the decisive feature in these systems was the construction costs. Table 1.1 compares the estimated costs per mile of a number of railways constructed in Shropshire at this time with known ropeway costs; ropeways came out at around a quarter of the cost of railways.

The first ropeway was built to carry coal to a pumping plant from a railway siding at Cosford in 1906. All the other major ropeways were connected to mines or quarries. The first of these linked Catherton Quarry with the Cleobury Mortimer and Ditton Priors Light Railway in 1908; by the time of the First World War it had been joined by systems at Bayton and Billingsley, although the former ran for most of its course in Worcestershire. The Stipperstones' systems constructed in the period at the very end of the First World War and into the early 1920s brought an end to this phase of ropeway building. Indeed, after the Second World War with the closure of the Huglith line, it must have seemed that the days of aerial ropeways in the county were over. However, this reckoned without their popularity with the National Coal Board as a way of moving coal and spoil within colliery sites instead of long, rope-worked, tramways. Thus the final ropeway in the county was built at Alveley Colliery in 1960. When the colliery closed in 1969 it brought to an end the age of aerial ropeways in Shropshire.

Table 1.1 Comparative costs of aerial ropeways and railways in Shropshire, c1910

Date	System	Cost/Mile
1900	Cleobury Mortimer and Ditton Priors Light Railway	£7,209
1907	Stottesdon, Kinlet and Billingsley Light Railway	£4,422
1913	Billingsley Colliery Railway	£8,000
	Average Railway	**£6,534**
1911	Bayton Colliery Ropeway	£1,575
1914	Billingsley Colliery Ropeway	£1,955
	Average Ropeway	**£1,765**

Costs are for construction of standard gauge lines. Whilst narrow gauge would be cheaper, there would be additional costs for engines and rolling stock; there was no equivalent expense for ropeways.

---

1 A.G. Keller, A Theatre of Machines, Jarrold, Norwich, 1964, pg 109; Encyclopedia Britannica, 1911, Conveyors (www.unz.org/Pub/Britannica-1911v07-00052).
2 A.J. Wallis-Tayler, Aerial or Wire-rope Tramways, Crosby-Lockwood, London, 1898, Pp 7, 217; R.A. Trennert, Riding the High Wire: Aerial Mine Tramways in the West, University Press of Colorado, 2002, Pp5-28. The first application for a patent in Britain for a ropeway was in 1856 by Henry Robinson of Settle, but Hodgson's system was the first to make any impact.
3 Wallis Tayler, Pg 7; www.hoistmagazine.com/features/historic-hoists/
   Hodgson had considered twin cable systems but settled on the single rope system.
4 Britannica, Conveyors.
5 Wallis-Tayler, Pg 153
6 T. Donnelly, Structural and technical change in the Aberdeen Quarrying Industry, 1830-1880; Industrial Archaeology Review, 3, 1979, Pp 229-238.
7 K. Beddoes and W. Smith, The Cleobury Mortimer and Ditton Priors Light Railway, Oxford Publishing, 1981, Pg 12.

Part 1: East Shropshire

2. The Catherton Aerial Ropeway

The Catherton ropeway ran for approximately 3½ miles from Catherton Quarry on the eastern slopes of the Titterstone Clee Hill (SO 613777) to Detton Sidings on the Cleobury Mortimer and Ditton Priors Light Railway (SO 663797) (Figure 2.1). The quarry and the ropeway both owed their existence to the railway.

Large scale quarrying of basalt (known locally as basalt) began on the Clee Hill in about 1863 with the formation of the Dhustone Quarry Company. This operated a quarry on the west of the hill (Figure 2.2); it used the recently constructed Ludlow and Clee Hill Railway to send its stone away. The latter reached the top of the Clee Hill, by a long, self-acting, standard-gauge inclined plane. It was followed by the Clee Hill Granite Company c1872 and the Titterstone Quarry of Messrs Field and Mackay in 1881.[1] These also operated on the west of the hill, taking advantage of the rail link to Ludlow and thence to the national railway network. There were substantial reserves of basalt on the east of the hill, but no easy way of reaching them. A narrow-gauge tramway was built over the top of the hill to reach a coal mine in 1872 but both it and the mine were abandoned a few years later.[2] It was not until the promotion of a light railway between Cleobury Mortimer and Ditton Priors in 1900 that serious thought was given to quarrying at Catherton. This line would allow a ready outlet for any quarry on the east of the hill. It seems that initial plans were for a rail link from Oreton on the light railway up the eastern slopes of the hill and continuing over the top to make a junction with the existing line coming up from Ludlow.[3] However, the construction of the railway did not begin until 1907 and by this time the proposed Oreton branch had been dropped. In 1905 the Clee Hill Granite Company obtained quarrying rights to the dhustone on the estate of Admiral Woodward at Catherton, and in August 1907 the company approached Woodward for permission to build an aerial ropeway over his land.[4]

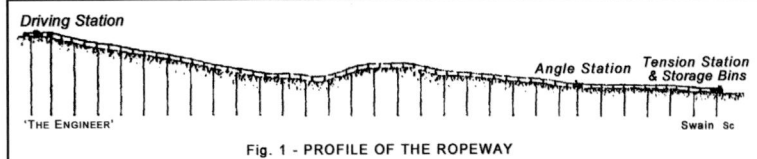

Figure 2.1a, above:
The Catherton ropeway elevation.
(The Engineer)

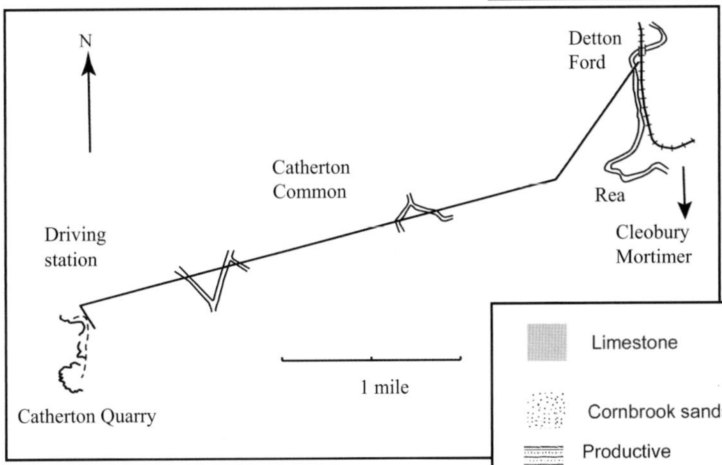

Figure 2.1b, left:
Map of the route of the Catherton ropeway.

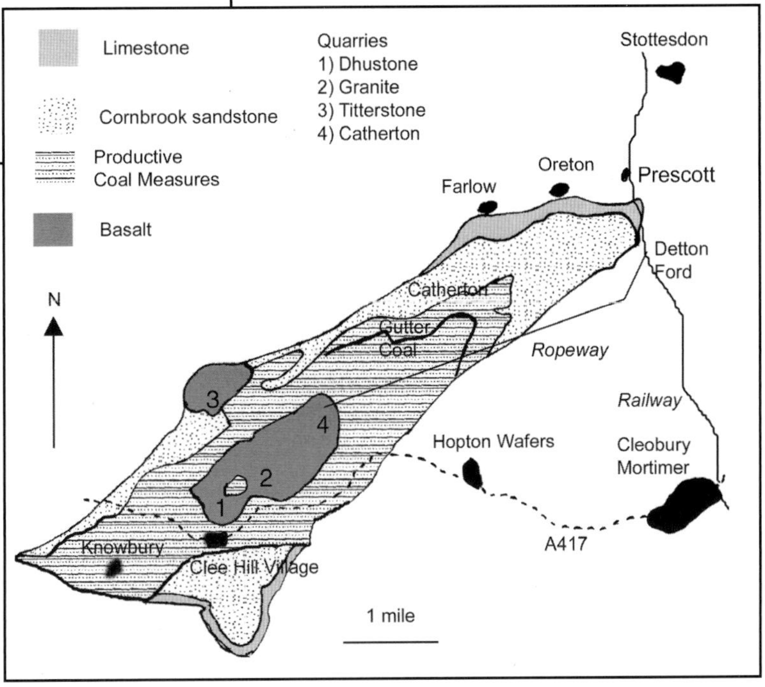

Figure 2.2, right:
Quarries on the Titterstone Clee Hill

SCMC Account 28 - Aerial Ropeways of Shropshire

Work on laying out Catherton Quarry began in 1908. In March of that year Thomas Lee Roberts on behalf of the quarry company signed a lease for the construction of the aerial ropeway terminus on land by Detton Mill and also entered into an agreement with the railway for connection of the siding.[5] The contract for the ropeway was awarded to J.M. Henderson of Aberdeen and it was laid out by their engineer, Mr G.F. Grover. Henderson's had pioneered the use of aerial ropeways at the granite quarries around Aberdeen and so were vastly experienced. Roberts paid the railway company for the siding connection in October 1908, probably marking the date that construction work started in earnest. By the time of the inspection of the railway for passenger traffic in November, the ropeway pylons had been erected and it was opened in February 1909. Alexander Mackie of Henderson's was the site engineer responsible for supervising construction of the ropeway and when the contract was complete he was retained by the Clee Hill Granite Company to supervise their railway, before moving in 1910 to a job in Bangalore.[6]

An extensive technical description of the ropeway was subsequently published by the Engineer.[7] The system used a single rope for both suspension and haulage, 1" in diameter. This was obtained locally from Edge's of Shifnal and brought to the site on four drums. The sections were joined by splices, each fifty feet in length. The driving station was at the quarry (Figure 2.3). Henderson's supplied a twin cylinder, inverted compound steam engine (high pressure cylinder 8", low pressure cylinder 14", stroke 18") which powered a 10' diameter winding wheel, 17'6" above the ground, via gearing. The engine was supplied with steam at 120 psi by a locomotive type boiler, 16'3" x 3'. The drive to the rope was activated by a friction clutch. The driving wheel had two grooves, both lagged with hardwood and the main rope ran in one of these. The rope itself was carried on 55 steel trestles, each made of four steel legs set in concrete. The maximum spacing between trestles was 350' and they were between 30' and 58' high, to ensure a minimum clearance of loaded buckets of 14' from the ground. The rope was carried on four 20" pulleys on the loaded side and two on the empties side. Each trestle had a ladder to allow access for oiling (Figure 2.4).

Figure 2.3a:
Driving station at Catherton Quarry
(R. Handley).

Figure 2.3b:
William Cleeton with an engine at Catherton Quarry. William was the younger brother of Ben Cleeton, who is remembered as driving the ropeway and William was also an engine driver. Based on the appearance of this machine, there is a good chance that it is the engine that drove the ropeway.
(E. Evans).

Figure 2.4: Aerial ropeway pylons near the quarry. The picture shows that not all the traffic to and from the quarry used the ropeway!
(E. Evans)

Figure 2.5: Angle Station *(R. Handley)*

Figure 2.6: Ropeway terminus. This picture is one of a pair showing Detton Ford and the new road bridge, built in 1926. Note the shunting horse. The post-man is Simon Evans, a noted writer of his day
(E. Evans/Beddoes and Smith)

Figure 2.7:
Ropeway terminus, 1909.

The object resembling a telephone box just in front of the hoppers is the counterweight which was attached to the return wheel to keep the rope taught.

The wheel can be seen on the gantry above, in its sliding frame.
(R. Handley)

Three miles from the quarry was an angle station, where the rope turned through an angle of 143° (Figure 2.5). At Detton Sidings was the return wheel of the ropeway and also the unloading bunkers (Figures 2.6, 2.7). A shunt rail lifted the buckets clear of the rope. The return wheel was positioned on a frame, allowing it to be slid back for a distance of up to 37'6"; this was to maintain tension in the rope as it gradually stretched with use. Once on the shunt rails, the buckets were moved manually to the discharge hopper. This was 63' long by 32'6" wide and was divided into six compartments (bins) by wooden partitions. By disconnecting a clip, the buckets could be turned upside down and the stone emptied into the appropriate bin (Figure 2.8). The structure stood on pillars over twin railway tracks so that wagons could run underneath it; by opening doors in the bottom of the bins, the stone could be loaded into the wagons. A third railway track ran along the east side of the hopper; chutes on either ends of the hopper allowed some types of stone to be loaded directly into wagons on this line. It is likely that stone setts (large blocks of stone used as cobbles for road surfaces) were loaded in this way. The sidings were the property of the Clee Hill Granite Company. A horse was used to shunt their wagons as the locomotives of the railway company were not allowed to enter the sidings. The ropeway buckets, once emptied, would be run round the shunt rail to its far end and then clipped back onto the rope. The total length of the discharge station was 230', with the discharge platform 45' above the ground.

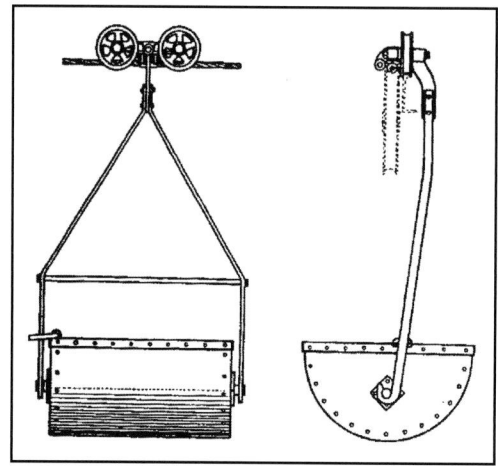

Figure 2.8: Ropeway bucket.
(Beddoes and Smith)

The empty buckets would eventually arrive back at the driving station at the quarry, where they would automatically be detached from the rope by a shunt rail. They of course needed to be refilled with stone. This was done by a short secondary ropeway, 230 yards long, which lead to the crushers (Figure 2.9). The rope for this was worked off the same driving wheel as the main ropeway, running in the second groove (see above). Thus the empty buckets would run along the shunt rail to the secondary ropeway and thence to the crushers. Here there were a number of shunt rails, allowing the buckets to be manually detached and filled with the appropriate grade of crushed stone or setts. Once this had been done, they were reattached to the secondary ropeway and carried back to the driving station. Here, they were led via another shunt rail back onto the main rope.

Figure 2.9: The secondary ropeway, running in front of the crushers. *(R. Handley)*

The quarry itself had a pair of Marsden jaw crushers; R.H. Marsden had a pedigree in making crushers almost as long as Henderson's in ropeway construction. Stone was brought to the crushers from the quarry face by a narrow-gauge tramway. It is said that Henderson's installed the crushing plant. With their experience in supplying the granite quarries around Aberdeen, they would be well-qualified for this work and no doubt it would have been financially advantageous to offer a combined contract for the ropeway and the quarry machinery. Indeed, this may have been an important factor in the decision to install an aerial ropeway.

Once completed, the ropeway was subject to a capacity trial, which apparently showed it could move 60 tons of stone an hour from the quarry to the Detton sidings; the quarry was considered to be capable of producing a maximum of 600 tons of stone a day (ie 180,000 tons pa). It seems unlikely that the ropeway ever carried anything like that. Unfortunately only total freight tonnages are reported for the railway; these are fragmentary and include the outputs for both Catherton and the Abdon Quarry at Ditton. However, if the outputs of both quarries were similar (and they were similarly sized), Catherton probably produced around 35,000 tons in 1910, 60,000 tons in 1913 and 50,000 tons in 1919. Peak output was probably in the First World War, with a slow decline thereafter. Even if the quarry operated at peak capacity, an output of 180,000 tons would not have been possible due to the limited capacity of the railway. This was limited to trains of 12 loaded wagons at a time; probably 120 tons a trip. In practice trains of 20 wagons were common, but it was still normal for wagons to be left uncollected. The storage bins could hold around 1,500 tons. Photographs of the sidings in use show that large quantities of stone simply dumped on the ground. Some of this may have been stockpiles that could not be accommodated elsewhere[8].

The ropeway and assorted operations needed a significant workforce. In the 1911 census, David Price of Oreton, aged 30 and Fred Evans, 21, of Creamer Gutter, both described themselves as aerial ropeway workers; Fred's father, Thomas, 48, a retired policeman, drove a stationary engine for the Clee Hill Granite Company and this may have been the engine for the ropeway. A fuller picture of the labour force comes from around 1920. At the quarry, the ropeway engine was driven by Ben Cleeton. Sam Morris and Albert Sutton worked at the angle station with Sam Pugh also employed to patrol the length of the ropeway to report or deal with problems. At Detton during this period the foreman was first Mr Chidley and then Bill Price. Edwin Martin, Tom Burton, Tom Duce, Bert Key, Bill George, Henry Gilson and George Broom worked on the discharge, with Tom Breakwell employed as a rope splicer and Arthur Lewis the shunter in charge of the horse. The clerk in the office was Mr. Bayfield[9].

The late Ben Crowther was employed as an oiler, together with Tom Wall, Archie Webb, Tom Gilson, George Breakwell and Sam Bishop. He recollected having to climb each ropeway pylon to oil the wheels that carried the rope; this could involve crawling along a 4" wide girder to reach the oiling points. He would be able to do around half the total number of pylons each day; about 28. Not surprisingly he sometimes rode in the buckets. Travelling at 5 mph, this gave plenty of time to do the oiling as he passed each pylon. However, the practice was frowned upon, with good reason. One day, the ropeway broke down, with Mr Crowther in a bucket halfway between two pylons.

> "So they said 'Crowther's trapped in a bucket'. Well, I didn't fancy waiting until they fixed the ropeway. I had some bailer-twine in my pocket. I tied this to the bucket and took hold of the other end of it. Then I jumped…"

Needless to say, the twine promptly broke. Fortunately, Mr Crowther landed in fern and was unhurt. He was not the only member of his family to have a narrow escape on the ropeway. An uncle, employed at the discharge station, fell into one of the loading bins. He also escaped unhurt[10].

Whilst stone was the main traffic on the ropeway, it would also have been used to transport some supplies to the quarry. In the First World War, it is said that some coal slack was sent down it, from the pits on the hill. This may have come from reworking of the spoil tips of disused collieries.[11] Female labour is also said to have been used on the ropeway at this time.

After the War, a concrete block-making plant was opened at Detton, to use the fine dust that could not otherwise be sold. A similar concrete plant at Abdon had been extremely successful. Unfortunately it said that the Detton plant failed due to lack of water.[12] Catherton Quarry began to struggle in the 1920s. The market for stone setts fell away as road-makers turned to tarred stone. A new cracker was installed to produce more of the finely crushed stone that was now needed. However, less could be done about geological problems. Attempts to open a second face to the north of the original quarry appear to have been unsuccessful. Whilst a second face to the south was developed, it eventually ran into faults, leading to problems producing marketable stone. The quarry closed in 1928 and the ropeway stopped running. The rope was quickly sold for scrap, but the discharge terminus was not dismantled until the Second World War.[13]

The Remains

Today, many of the pylon bases of the ropeway survive, especially on the common land of the Clee Hill. One is marked with the date 1908 (Figures 2.10, 2.11). A sheave wheel from a pylon survives; it was made by Hadfield's of Sheffield (Figure 2.12). At Detton a number of pylon bases are still in-situ. The office still stands and the track-bed of the sidings and the railway are obvious.

Figure 2.10:
Base of aerial ropeway at Catherton Common carrying date (SO 64127829).

The measuring rod is marked in 6" sections.
(D.Poyner)

Figure 2.11 (below):
Base of aerial ropeway pylon, Catherton Common (SO 64247832). The supports for the ropeway were made of angle iron, concreted directly into each of the four bases. *(D.Poyner)*

At Catherton, the quarries are prominent. The field evidence for the crushers and ropeway pose some questions. There are two crusher complexes, one approximately 100 yards from the ropeway driving station, another about 200 yards away. This is consistent with the description of the secondary ropeway as being 230 yards long. The first set of crushers undoubtedly date from the start of the quarry as they are illustrated in the 1912 article in "The Engineer". The second set appear more recent (the surviving structures are entirely made from concrete, as opposed the mixture of concrete and dhustone blocks used for the first crushers). This suggests that the terminus of the secondary ropeway was redeveloped, perhaps around 1920.[14] A photograph exists of the return wheel with tensioning weight (Figure 2.13).

Figure 2.12:
Sheave wheel from the aerial ropeway, once used as reinforcing for a concrete base. *(D.Poyner)*

Figure 2.13:
Return wheel of secondary ropeway with weights to provide tension. *(Shropshire Archives, PH/C/21/3/37)*

---

1. P.B. Hewitt, Basalt quarrying in the Cleehill region of South Shropshire. Tarmac Papers, III, (1999), Pp 273-300.
2. Shropshire Archives (SA), 5216/2/G2-3
3. SA 5216/2/G5
4. The lease of the land for the aerial ropeway terminal (below) in 1908 recites a lease of 1905 giving rights to work dhustone under the Woodward estate; this date is consistent with the description of the Clee Hill Granite Company in the Mining Year Book for 1916 (Pg 151). A letter in the Hopton Court archives from Keary and Willey, solicitors to Admiral Woodward, 2-8-1907, is the first mention of the aerial ropeway.
5. Lease, Woodward to Roberts, Hopton Court deeds; K. Beddoes and W. Smith, The Cleobury Mortimer and Ditton Priors Light Railway, Oxford Publishing Company, (1982), Pg 30
6. Beddoes and Smith, 30; A.E. Jenkins, Titterstone Clee Hill; Everyday Life, Industrial History and Dialect, privately published, (1982), Pp 31-6.
7. Anon, An aerial ropeway for a Shropshire Quarry, The Engineer, Jan 26th 1912, Pp 89-90, 96.
8. Beddoes and Smith, Pp 23, 36, 110
9. Beddoes and Smith, Pg 53
10. Interview, Mr B. Crowther, Dec 1996.
11. Beddoes and Smith, Pg 39.
12. Beddoes and Smith, Pg 53
13. Beddoes and Smith, Pg 57
14. D. Poyner, Catherton Quarry, Cleobury Chronicles, 8, (2008), Pp 17-27

3. Bayton Ropeway

The Bayton ropeway ran for a little over a mile from the Bayton Colliery (SO 697734) to Cleobury Mortimer station (SO 702753) on the Tenbury and Bewdley Railway (Figure 3.1). Bayton Colliery was developed by James Smallshaw, a coal owner from Shrewsbury, in the early 20th century. It worked coal under the Shakenhurst estate at Bayton.[1] To the east this was bounded by the much larger Mawley estate of Sir Walter Blount. The coal reserves accessible under the Shakenhurst estate from Smallshaw's colliery were enough to last about 15 years, but there were much larger reserves beneath the Mawley estate. Whilst the Bayton Colliery was worth developing, in the medium to long term the future of mining in the area inevitably lay under the Mawley estate.

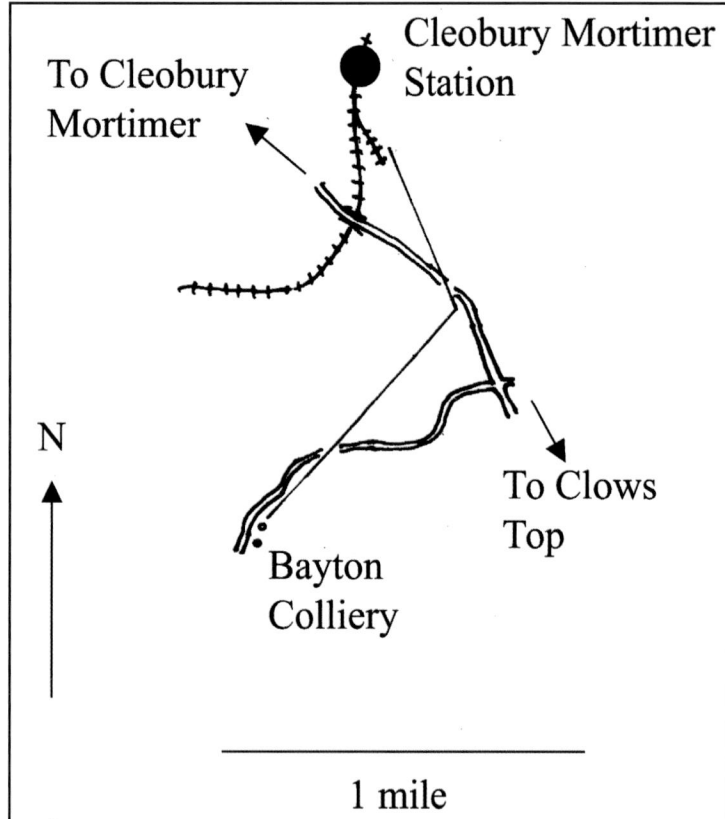

Figure 3.1a, left:
Bayton ropeway location map.

Figure 3.1b, below:
Bayton ropeway section.

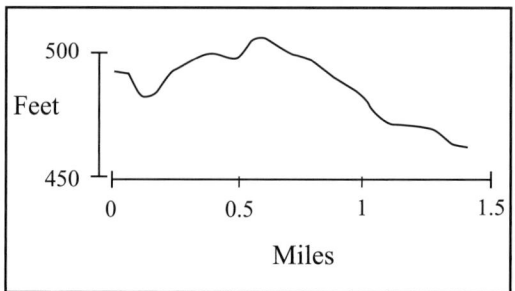

Smallshaw initially had great plans for his mine at Bayton, but they relied on access to the nearest railway to carry the coal away. In 1907 he was granted permission to build a tramroad from the mine to Cleobury Mortimer station on the Great Western-owned railway from Bewdley to Woofferton Junction. However, he never developed this and the pit remained small, employing around 30 men and with a traction engine to haul coal.[2] He sold it in 1911 to Francis Whitworth Wright, a mining engineer from Huddersfield but by this date living locally at Pensax.[3] Wright obviously shared Smallshaw's assessment that the mine needed a rail outlet, but his solution was an aerial ropeway. He approached R. White and Sons to design a system for him.[4] White's were experienced ropeway engineers, specialising in both aerial and surface systems; perhaps their most high-profile contract had been the construction of the Great Orme Tramway at Llandudno at the turn of the century.

The ground between the colliery and Cleobury Mortimer station was easily graded and there would have been no problem in constructing a railway. Whilst Wright might have had problems in getting a way-leave from the Mawley estate for the construction of a railway, the most likely reason that he opted for a ropeway was probably the lower construction costs. Bayton was never going to produce particularly large amounts of coal and so a ropeway would have ample capacity for his needs. White's had considerable experience in constructing colliery ropeways, in much the same way that Henderson's were associated with quarrying and hoists for engineering projects.

In August 1911 Wright entered into an agreement with the Great Western Railway for a connection between their line at Cleobury and proposed colliery sidings and in October of that year he was given permission by Shropshire County Council for the ropeway, subject to the erection of a safety net or bridge where the line crossed the road to Clows Top. The latter was necessary if the ropeway was to run in a straight line between the colliery and the station. It was hardly an onerous request but for reasons explained below, this was not acceptable to White's. The line was altered so that the road was crossed in Worcestershire, where the County Council did not require any additional safety measures. As a consequence, an angle station was necessary close to the road, where the rope turned through 104½° (SO 705743). The ropeway inevitably crossed over the land of the Mawley estate for most of its course. The formal agreement with the estate was signed in April 1912 and the ropeway was soon constructed. The ropeway cost around £2,100, with a further £1,100 spent on the rail connection at Cleobury Mortimer station and around £250 on a screening plant for coal at the colliery.[5]

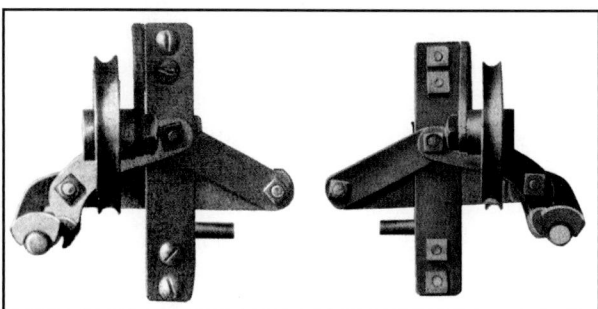

Figure 3.3, above: White's patent clip as used on the ropeway buckets with the gripper open (left) and closed (right).

Figure 3.2, above: Aerial ropeway pylon.

Figure 3.4: Pithead, Bayton Colliery, c1911.

The total length of the ropeway was 7,030' (ie $1^{1}/_{3}$ miles) and it was carried on steel pylons 25' to 50' high, similar in design to those of the Catherton ropeway (Figure 3.2). For White's it marked a new departure as it was a single rope system and the company used a new design of clip to grip the rope (Figure 3.3). They claimed that the gripper would work on gradients as steep as 1 in 1 and was not affected by ice or excess lubricant. It also allowed automatic operation, without the need for manual detaching. It seems likely that White's intended Bayton to be a show-piece for their new system, explaining their reluctance to install the safety nets requested by Shropshire County Council. The ropeway was featured in Engineering in May 1913, when it was noted that "it has not been considered necessary to provide safety bridges at these points. Reliance has been placed on the grip of the rope saddles". White's probably considered these sentences were worth the expense of constructing an angle station and promptly reprinted the article as one of their publicity brochures![6]

At the colliery, coal was wound up the upcast shaft. The cages were landed on a stage about nine feet above ground level and then trammed along a gantry, over a weighbridge before being emptied onto a jigging screen (Figure 3.4). This was powered by a small single-cylinder steam engine and sorted the coal into 4 grades according to their size. The different grades fell into distinct compartments in a storage bunker, constructed by White's. On the other side of the bunker was the driving station of the ropeway (Figure 3.5). The buckets, resting on a shunt rail, were fed via eight chutes and then attached to the rope. This was driven from a horizontal wheel.[7] The power source for this is not clear. It has been said that it was driven via shafts and gearing by the winding engine for the downcast shaft, a horizontal cross-compound made by Pearcy and Co. As the downcast was not used for coal winding, this would be an economical use of power. However, an inventory taken of the pit at the end of 1914 indicates that the downcast winder was an apparently simple twin cylinder engine, 6" diameter and 12" stroke, geared to the winding drum. This does not sound like the Pearcy machine. The inventory gives no clues as to the engine that powered the ropeway. It is possible that the Pearcy engine replaced the 1914 winder.[8]

The angle station was of simple design (Figure 3.6). The ropes passed round large diameter wheels set horizontally whilst the buckets ran on shunt rails. There was a landsale yard at the angle station, presumably with an eye for traffic on the nearby road from Cleobury, although in 1914 the weighing machine here was considered scrap. Also at the angle station were a hand crab and a spare wheel, both "broken", suggesting it was treated as something of a junk yard. There were chains and lifting gear that did seem to be functional, as well as spare clips for the buckets.[9]

At Cleobury Mortimer station, the company had their own sidings, connected to the Great Western sidings (Figure 3.7). The ropeway terminal was very similar to the driving station; essentially a 76' long U-shaped shunt rail to take the buckets whilst the rope ran around a return wheel (Figure 3.8). Weights on the return wheel ensured that the rope was kept under tension. The buckets emptied into three chutes that allowed a similar number of railway wagons to be filled simultaneously. The terminus was connected to the angle station and the driving station by telephone.[10] It seems that empty wagons were delivered to the sidings by Great Western locomotives which could work up to 112 yards over the Bayton company's rails. There were three empties sidings with a nominal capacity of 40 wagons. When they were ready to be filled, they would gravitate to the discharge point on the ropeway terminus and thence over a weighbridge to await collection by the Great Western engine. There was space for up to 20 full wagons.[11] A small galvanised iron cabin was provided. The colliery company had its own wagons. It is said that it purchased some wagons second hand from the Great Western but much of its early stock was on hire-purchase from the British Wagon Company and the Lincoln Wagon Company. The company cash books also record occasional payments to the Midland Railway and Carriage Works, the North Central Wagon Company and the Gloucester Wagon Works; in 1922-3 payments were made to the South Staffordshire Wagon Company.[12]

Once established the ropeway led an uneventful life. It was designed to deliver 35 tons an hour[13]; in practice it probably never exceeded 20% of this capacity. In the first year of its life it delivered around 8,300 tons of coal to Cleobury station. The output of the colliery was around 10,000 tons pa.[14] The lease that allowed the ropeway to pass over the Mawley estate specified a payment of ½d for every ton that was carried, with a minimum payment of £30pa; equivalent to carriage of 14,400 tons pa. It was in the interest of the company to carry more coal, to reduce the average cost of transport per ton; however, they never seem to have achieved this.[15] The cash books reveal significant expenditure on the ropeway in 1917 and 1918. In June 1917 over £50 was paid to "White" and "R. White", probably the ropeway makers. In December 1917 and again in December 1918 a total of over £100 was paid to British Ropeway Engineering for undisclosed services. In August 1918 "Glover" was paid £502. This latter item was almost certainly to Messrs Glover Brothers of Mossley, Lancashire, makers of wire ropes. The old rope was replaced in 1918 as it had become worn.[16]

Glover Brothers were closely associated with British Ropeway Engineering and it looks like between them the two companies were responsible for repair and maintenance of the ropeway. Small payments to British Ropeways Engineering continued to be made throughout the rest of the life of the ropeway and in 1920 another £80 was paid to Glover's, although this may reflect purchase of winding or haulage ropes for other operations about the colliery.

Figure 3.5:
Screens and ropeway loading station.

Figure 3.6: Angle Station.

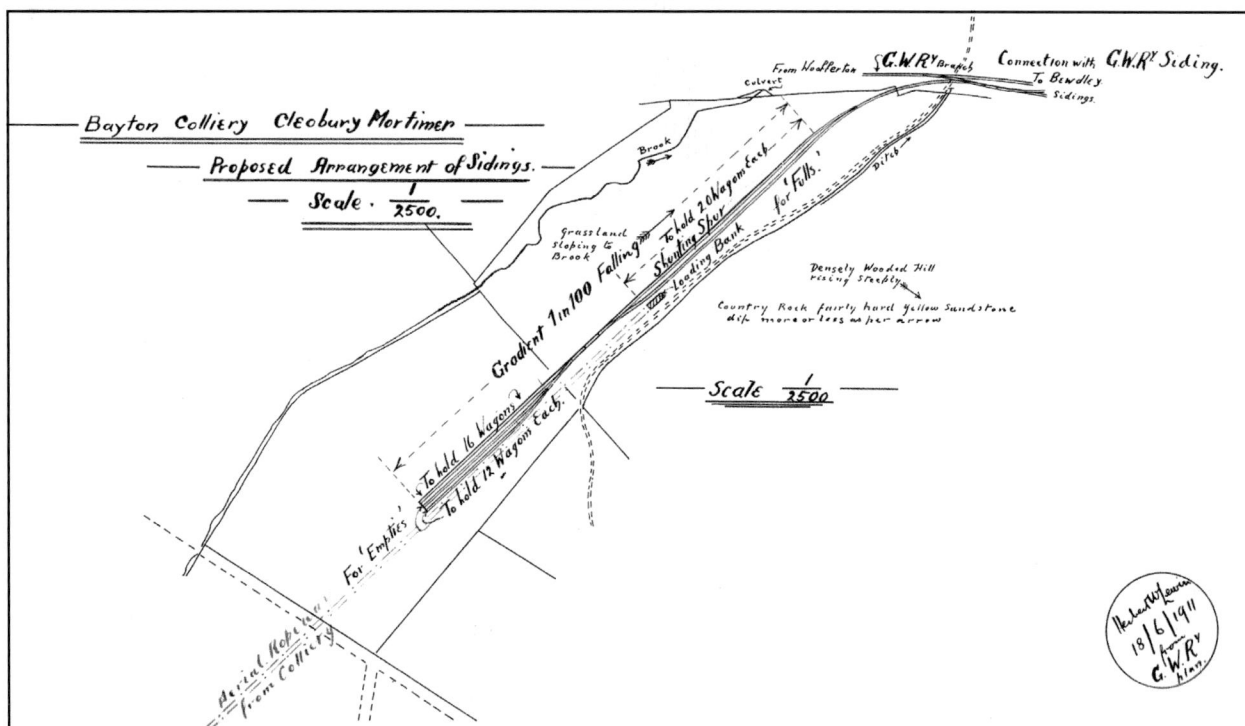

Figure 3.7: Plan of proposed sidings at Cleobury Mortimer Station.

Figure 3.8:
Discharge terminus, Cleobury Mortimer Station.

Whilst the ropeway went peacefully about its business, more dramatic events were taking place elsewhere and these were to have a bearing on its fate. In 1914 Wright not only obtained a way-leave agreement with the Mawley estate for the ropeway, he was also given first refusal on the option of the mineral rights under the estate. To take full advantage of this he needed more financial backing. He was introduced to Ernest and Vincent Bramall, colliery owners with significant interests in Lancashire and Leicestershire. Together the three formed the Bayton Colliery Company, in December 1914. However, the outbreak of war four months earlier prevented any further negotiations with the Mawley estate; Sir Walter Blount and Wright both took active parts in the fighting. It was not until 1919 that discussions with the Mawley estate resumed and agreement was not reached until April 1921.[17] No significant investment had taken place at Bayton since the purchase of the ropeway, as it had always been assumed that it would be replaced by a new sinking on the Mawley lands and as a result, by 1921 it was in terminal decline.

With their new lease, the Bayton Colliery Company lost no time in starting work on a new sinking. Its location was determined principally by the ropeway; it was envisaged that this would be used to send the coal from the new pit to the railway and so the shafts had to be in an easy line with the existing terminal. Consequently, a site was chosen just outside Mamble village, about a mile from Bayton Colliery. Unfortunately, as soon as the shaft reached the coal it became obvious that it was unworkable; it suffered very badly from influx of water. The sinking was abandoned in 1922. By June 1923, conditions had also become intolerable at Bayton and that too was forced to close. Needless to say, the ropeway stopped running. Within a few months, the company found workable coal on the Mawley estate, around 2½ miles from Bayton. This quickly developed into a profitable mine. At this point, the company discovered that in 1920s Britain, a rail link was no longer needed. With the development of petrol engines, the colliery was able to flourish relying on landsale to lorries. Indeed, in 1926 it started direct delivery to customers and its road haulage arm became the most profitable part of the business.[18]

The ropeway was not demolished until 1938, although it must have been obvious for years before that it was never going to be used again. Sir Walter Blount, on hearing of the demolition, requested that one pylon be retained as a shooting platform on his estate but this was turned down. The railway sidings saw occasional use in the 1920s after the ropeway stopped running, but in 1931 the company built a brickworks on the site of the discharge terminus. This worked until 1964. Today, the most obvious survival of the ropeway is the base of the angle station; the massive concrete pier that held the guide wheels defied all attempts at destruction.[19]

---

1. For the history of Bayton Colliery see R. Evans and D. Poyner, The Wyre Forest Coalfield, Tempus, Stroud, 2000, Pp 125-142.
2. Keith Beddoes, Bayton Colliery and its aerial ropeway, Journal 1978. Shrops. Caving & Mining Club, 1978, Pp 55-60
3. Sale, Smallshaw to Wright, 1911, authors' collection
4. Beddoes, op. cit.
5. Beddoes, op. cit.; lease GWR to Wright, 1911; lease Mawley estate to Wright, 1912; valuation of Bayton Colliery, 1914: all authors' collection
6. Aerial ropeway at Bayton Colliery, Engineering, May 16th 1913, Pg 670, reprinted with additional photographs as R. White brochure 102. The late Geoffrey Bramall, who latterly ran the Bayton Colliery Company was unimpressed by the ropeway and in his copy of the brochure, wrote "not strictly true" next to the claim that the gripper was unaffected by frost, snow or excess lubricant. Mr Bramall claimed that the company had to purchase slack from the neighbouring Hollins Colliery to power the driving engine for the ropeway, the angle station caused large spillages of coal and that latterly the ropeway's chief proponent was the company's marketing manager. This was probably Sidney Chitham, the sales and marketing manager. As Chitham is likely to have relayed on rail dispersals for most of his sales, it is not implausible he was strongly in favour of the ropeway. Before motor haulage became an easy option, it is difficult to imagine that the colliery could have managed without the ropeway, whatever its technical problems.
7. White brochure
8. Beddoes, op. cit., quoting Mr. G. Bramall; Bayton valuation, op. cit.
9. White brochure
10. White brochure
11. Beddoes and W.H. Smith, The Tenbury and Bewdley Railway, Wild Swan Publications, Didcot, 1995, Pp 70-3
12. Beddoes, op. cit.; Cash Books, Bayton Colliery Company, 1915-1918, 1918-1922, 1922-27, authors collection.
13. White brochure,
14. Beddoes op. cit.; Kidderminster Times 8-1-1916, 8-7-1916; balance sheets Bayton Colliery Co, 1919, 1922, authors' collection
15. Lease, GWR to Wright; cash books (royalty payments to Mawley estate/Blount)
16. Beddoes, op. cit.
17. Lease, Mawley Estate to Bayton Colliery Company, 1921
18. Notes of the late G. Bramall, authors collection
19. Beddoes, op. cit.

4. Billingsley Ropeway

The Billingsley ropeway was a short-lived venture that ran from Billingsley Brickworks (SO 706 850) to the Billingsley Colliery screens at Priors Moor (SO 716 834), also the terminus for the private colliery railway that ran to the Severn Valley Railway (Figure 4.1).

The ropeway was built by the Billingsley Colliery Company although it owed its existence to a series of unplanned developments. The company was formed in 1910, to breathe new life into the small Billingsley Colliery. The latter was sunk 40 years before amidst considerable fanfare but had quickly passed into obscurity. The principle factor in its revival was to be the construction of a rail link. Initially this was planned to be the Cleobury Mortimer and Ditton Priors line, which was to be reached via a new branch; the Stottesdon, Kinlet and Billingsley Light Railway. In fact this never materialised and the company built its own connection to the Severn Valley line. The colliery itself was thoroughly modernised and the company also realised that it would need to build houses for the workers employed at the mine.[1] The colliery was sunk on land belonging to Lord Barnard and when plans for the houses were first drawn up, early in 1911, it was envisaged that they would be on the Barnard estate close to the colliery. There was a brickyard in Billingsley which had been operating since the 1860s and in October 1911 the company took over the lease for this.[2] However, that marked the end of progress. Barnard's land agent became ill and eventually died. The new agent wanted the company to build more houses than they thought necessary. It was also unclear how water would be brought to the new houses.

Figure 4.1a, right: Billingsley Colliery Ropeway section.

Figure 4.1b, below:
Billingsley Colliery Ropeway location map.

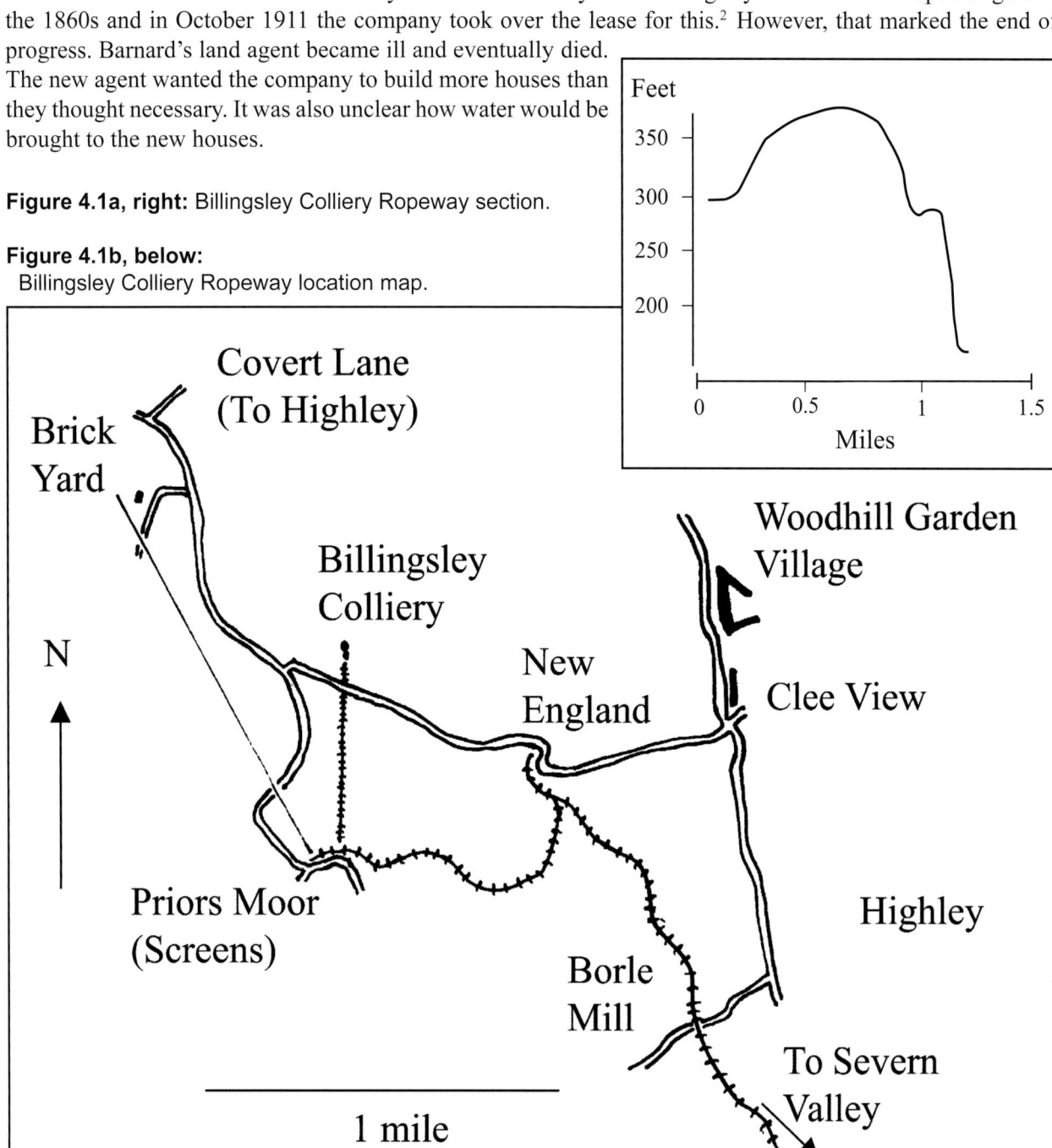

SCMC Account 28 - Aerial Ropeways of Shropshire

By the summer of 1912, the company had abandoned any hopes of building in Billingsley and turned instead to Highley, where there was already a sizeable settlement thanks to the efforts of the Highley Mining Company. In October 1912 they purchased 10½ acres of land in the north of the village and almost immediately began to build 35 houses.[3]

The company's brickyard in Billingsley was not ideally sited for the new building site. Whilst relatively short and direct road routes existed, using roads via New England or Covert Lane, neither was suited to heavy traffic. The surfaces were poor and the gradients up and down the valley of the Borle Brook were formidable. The company used local haulage contractors to move the 800,000 bricks required by horse, motor-tractor and traction engine. Bridgnorth District Council, the highway authority for the minor roads in Billingsley and Chelmarsh, sued the company for damage. That the council lost the case because the roads were in such a bad state prior to the movement of the bricks was to some extent a hollow victory; the company needed far more than 35 houses and the local roads were not up to the demands that would be put on them.[4]

In July 1913 work started on the main phase of house building; a Garden Village of 208 houses to the north of their previous estate, with Messrs Bowen of Marl Hill, Gloucester, as contractors.[5] A little before this, in April 1913, the colliery railway to Priors Moor had opened.[6] The problems of moving bricks remained as acute as ever and it was probably out of desperation that the company turned to an aerial ropeway to connect their brickyard with the railway terminus. It was not an ideal situation. Road haulage through Highley would still be needed to get the bricks from the station to Garden Village. However, Highley was in the territory of Cleobury Mortimer Rural District Council and so at least haulage along Bridgnorth District Council's roads would be avoided. In September 1913 the company applied for permission to Bridgnorth District Council for a ropeway to cross their minor road by the brickyard.[7] The application to Shropshire County Council for permission for the ropeway to cross the main Bridgnorth to Cleobury road (maintained by the County Council, not the District) was not made until December of that year, with authorisation coming the next month.[8]

An aerial ropeway was not, on the face of things, the simplest solution to the Billingsley Colliery Company's problems. The Billingsley Brickworks were around ¾ of a mile from their colliery; it would have been a simple matter to connect the two by means of a rope-worked tramway and then use the existing rail connection from the mine. There may have been issues with the Barnard Estate over wayleaves and the tramway would have needed to get across the Bridgnorth-Cleobury road, which would have added to its expense. It may also have been thought that the tramway that connected the colliery with the railway would not have the capacity to take both coal and bricks. For whatever reason, once the brickyard-colliery option had been ruled out, a ropeway became much more attractive. The railway was at a considerably lower height than the colliery and brickyard and an expensive incline would have had to be built to get the bricks down to the sidings. For what was probably only going to be a short-lived operation, a ropeway would have been much more cost-effective than such a tramway.

Figure 4.2:
The ropeway pylons approaching Prior's Moor.

The ropeway was built by Ropeways Ltd for a reported cost of £2,700.[9] It ran for just under 2,000 yards (approximately 1 1/8th miles) in a straight line. The pylons each had three legs mounted on concrete plinths via holding-down bolts (Figures 4.2, 4.3). This was a Ropeways Ltd design feature. The pylons had several large sheave wheels mounted on equalising beams to support the single rope; this transferred the weight of the buckets to the whole length of rope. The company engineer, John Pearce Roe held several patents relating to the design of supporting wheels and ropeway clips. The "Roe system" of ropeways was a conventional single rope design but which incorporated his various inventions. Roe claimed that it allowed a single rope to carry loads that normally would require a double rope; however, by the time of the Billingsley ropeway, single rope systems supported by multiple sheaves on equalising beams were common.[10]

Much of the technical design at Billingsley Colliery had been done by one of the directors, Edmund Mills Hann. Hann fulfilled a similar role at the massive Powell Duffryn company in South Wales, where he had a reputation for innovation. Hann and his son E.L. Hann made use of aerial ropeways at some of their collieries. At Bedwas Colliery, built at the same time as Billingsley, a twin-cable ropeway took coal from a bunker to the

Figure 4.3:
Aerial ropeway bases,

4.3a) base of the distant pylon in the wood, seen in Figure 4.2.
(D Poyner)

Figure 4.3:

4.3b) detail of single base near the brickyard (SO 7098 8446).

The concrete incorporates lumps of brick as rubble.

The measuring rod is marked in 6" sections.
(D Poyner)

Figure 4.4: Loading and tension station, Billingsley brickyard.

The late Ted Brick, a fitter, is next to the bucket, on the left.

Figure 4.5: Discharge and driving station, Billingsley Colliery Screens, Priors Moor.

View looking west.

Ted Brick is on the lower deck by the motor.

Figure 4.6: Discharge and driving station, Billingsley Colliery Screens, Priors Moor.

View looking east.

Ted Brick is at the bottom of the gantry. Mr Brick was still employed as a fitter when the aerial ropeway was installed at Alveley in 1960; he was unimpressed when it was suggested that this represented modern technology!

colliery boilers. At Bargoed, one ropeway took dirt to the mound and another moved coal to a coking plant. The first substantial aerial ropeway at any Welsh pit was built at Elliot Pit, New Tredegar, by Hann and for this he employed John Roe. It is likely that the decision to install a ropeway at Billingsley was taken by Hann.[11]

The buckets began their journey at the brickyard, where it seems bricks were loaded by hand (Figure 4.4). The buckets were of the normal side-tipping design. They were probably pushed off the shunt rail onto the rope by hand. The tension wheel was also at this end of the ropeway. This seems to be of a design peculiar to Ropeways Ltd. The wheel was attached to a winch which itself was capable of being turned by a vertically mounted rod, carefully balanced with weights. As the haulage rope became slack, so the tension decreased in the rope connecting the return wheel to the winch. The weighted rod would then move down, engaging with the winch and turning it so as to take up the slack and restore the tension.[12] The loaded buckets descended to the discharge station; where they passed over the main road there were nets to protect passing traffic from any spillages. The discharge station was built on a gantry over Bind Brook (Figures 4.5, 4.6). Once on the shunt rail, the bricks were emptied down a chute into a waiting railway wagon. The buckets were then pushed around the U-bend in the shunt rail. At this point they could be filled with coal slack, to go back to the brickyard to fire the kilns. At the foot of the discharge station was a concrete hopper into which slack could be emptied from railway wagons; the same wagon could then be shunted a few yards further down the track to receive the bricks. A conveyor picked up the slack from the hopper and took it up to the level of the buckets. As the discharge station was only a few yards from the coal screens (Figure 4.7), getting slack was easy. The electric motor that drove the ropeway was also mounted on the discharge station; power was brought to this from the colliery. It seems likely that two people normally worked on the discharge station, with perhaps two or three at the loading point at the brickyard.

Figure 4.7:
Billingsley Colliery Screens, Priors Moor.

Note ropeway terminus on the left, with the screens behind.

Figure 4.8:
The Mann steam cart, owned by haulage contractor Thomas Brick and used to haul bricks to Garden Village.

It is pictured in the 1930s, deep in retirement. It was probably purchased second hand from the Billingsley Colliery Company by Brick.

(The late N. Brick)

Once the bricks had been loaded into wagons, the problem remained of how to get them to the building site at Garden Village. It seems likely that the wagons were taken to either a headshunt on the railway at New England or a level crossing at Borle Mill. From there, the bricks could be unloaded and taken by horse and cart or steam lorry to Garden Village (Figure 4.8). Both routes would avoid using Bridgnorth District Council roads, other than the few yards needed to access the loading points. The New England road would be the shorter.

Whilst formal permissions for the ropeway all seem to have been in place by January 1914, construction seems to have been delayed for several months. There were problems with Messrs Bowen, the contractors at Garden Village. The job does not seem to have gone well for them. Within a month or so of them starting in late August, their labourers went on strike. Although this was probably settled quickly, other problems persisted and it seems that at the start of 1914 they gave the contract up.[13] It does not seem that it was until April that new contractors, Henry Smith and Sons of Wolverley could be found.[14] While this was going on, Ropeways Limited seem to have had problems of their own, with a shortage of steel hampering their progress.[15] Amongst the Ropeways Limited archives, there is one surviving drawing from 1914.[16] This was done on May 5th and shows a sheave with a spur wheel bolted on and a pinion. This is consistent with the driving arrangements used on the Billingsley ropeway and may indicate that the drive mechanism for the ropeway was being prepared at that time. The ropeway was certainly in use by the start of June 1914. The company gave £50 to the Bridgnorth District Council for road repairs but stated that they would not use New England again due to their "recently constructed" ropeway. The wording is consistent with the construction of the ropeway in May 1914.[17]

The ropeway may have saved the roads in Billingsley from damage but it was of no use for those in Highley. In December 1914 the company gave two loads of stone to Cleobury District Council for road repairs in Highley with another two promised. At the parish council in early 1915 it was noted that the road to Garden Village was to be repaired and the owner of the steam lorry apologised for the smoke from his wagon.[18] However, the state of the roads were the least of the Billingsley Colliery Company's problems as it entered 1915. It was in the middle of a protracted dispute with Cleobury District Council over the provision of sewage disposal facilities for the new houses. Until this was solved, there was little point in building further houses as the council would not give occupation licences for those that had already been built. It seems that all building stopped by May 1915.[19] Presumably at this point, the ropeway also stopped. With no houses, the Billingsley Colliery Company could not attract enough men to keep their mine going. Eventually they sold out to the Highley Mining Company. By June 1916 they had resumed work at Garden Village. However, the Highley company had their own brickyard in Highley and this was now used for the houses.[20] It seems unlikely that the ropeway was ever used again.

Figure 4.9:
Collapsed ropeway base from the discharge terminal at Priors Moor, showing how it is set in a concrete raft with tram rails as reinforcing.

The measuring rod is marked in 6" sections.
(D Poyner)

Figure 4.10:
Detail of ropeway base, showing how the holding down bolt was inserted after the bulk of the base had already been cast.

Below the base are the tram rails.

The measuring rod is marked in 6" sections.

(D Poyner)

Billingsley Colliery finally closed in September 1921. The ropeway was still standing at this point, but it was eventually dismantled. It is said that Billingsley Colliery Railway was used to move the scrap iron away.[21]

Today a few pylon bases survive. Those at the discharge station at the Billingsley screens are especially clear although they have recently collapsed into the brook. The slack bunker still survives. Above ground the pylon bases are simple 2' squares, raised 1' above the ground. However, at the discharge station they were set into a raft of concrete, 2' thick and below this were extended as 4' cubes into the ground. Furthermore, a pair of tram rails, set 18" apart was set into the concrete raft as reinforcing to link one base with another (Figures 4.9, 4.10).

---

1 For a review, see R. Evans and D. Poyner, The Wyre Forest Coalfield, Tempus, Stroud, 2000, Chapter 5, Pp 77-110.
2 Shropshire Archives (SA) Lease of Billingsley Brickyard
3 Staffordshire Record Office (StRO), D1230/Box 70/5
4 Bridgnorth Journal (BJ), 14-2-1914
5 Anon Diary 14-7-13, Derricutt Ledger August, both in private hands. Derricutt was a local builder
6 Public Record Office, MT6/2180/6
7 Anon Diary 25-8-13
8 5-12-13, 24-1-14 SCC Road and Bridges Committee; information ex-Keith Beddoes
9 BJ 6-6-14; the 1914 balance sheet valued the ropeway at £2200.
10 Ropeway at a Spanish Mine, The Engineer, May 22nd 1908, Pp 526-7, 528. "Conveyors", Encyclopedia Britannica, 1911.
11 E.M. Hann, The Mechanical Equipment of Collieries, Proceeding of the Institute of Mechanical Engineers, 71, 1906, Pp 719-50; E.L. Hann, The sinking and equipping of Bedwas Colliery, Colliery Garden, 106, 1913, Pp 473-8; Anon, Transactions of the Institution of Mining Engineers, Volume 116, 1956-7, Pg 429
12 The Engineer, op. cit.
13 BJ 13-9-13
14 Robinson Ledger 14-4-14, private hands
15 StRO, D1230/Box 70/5
16 Science Museum Library, ARCH ROP 8, Drawing 6289D, Order No E250.
17 BJ 6-6-14. The late Mrs Davies of the Brickyard House in Billingsley recalled an occasion in Billingsley when the local children were given rides in the buckets of the ropeway, which were decorated with flags and buntings. The celebrations are reminiscence of those for British Empire Day, celebrated around 24th May. It is possible that the ropeway was fit for use by this date and the event was used both to mark the empire and also the opening of the ropeway.
18 KT 12-12-14
19 This is the last date of any work done for Garden Village in the Derricutt ledgers.
20 BJ 10-6-16
21 J. Tennant, "The Billingsley and Kinlet Railways", Severn Valley News, Autumn 1974, 24, Pg 26

5. Alveley Colliery Ropeway

The Alveley Colliery ropeway was a short system that connected the pit head and shaft of Alveley Colliery (SO 753 842) with the coal screens in Highley, on the Severn Valley Railway (SO745 841) (Figure 5.1). It was the last ropeway to be built in Shropshire.

Alveley Colliery was sunk by the Highley Mining Company in the late 1930s; the workings of their mine in Highley had moved east under the Severn and it made sense to sink a new shaft close to where the faces were now found. However, this posed a problem as to get the coal away to markets required access to the Severn Valley railway, by then a branch of the Great Western Railway. This ran on the Highley bank of the Severn. The problem was solved by building a bridge over the river. Coal from the shaft was taken from the pit to the railway in tubs, running on an endless rope haulage. (The same tubs ran underground by a broadly similar rope haulage.) The coal was screened and graded at a plant built by the railway on the Highley side of the river. It was then loaded into wagons and taken away in trains.[1]

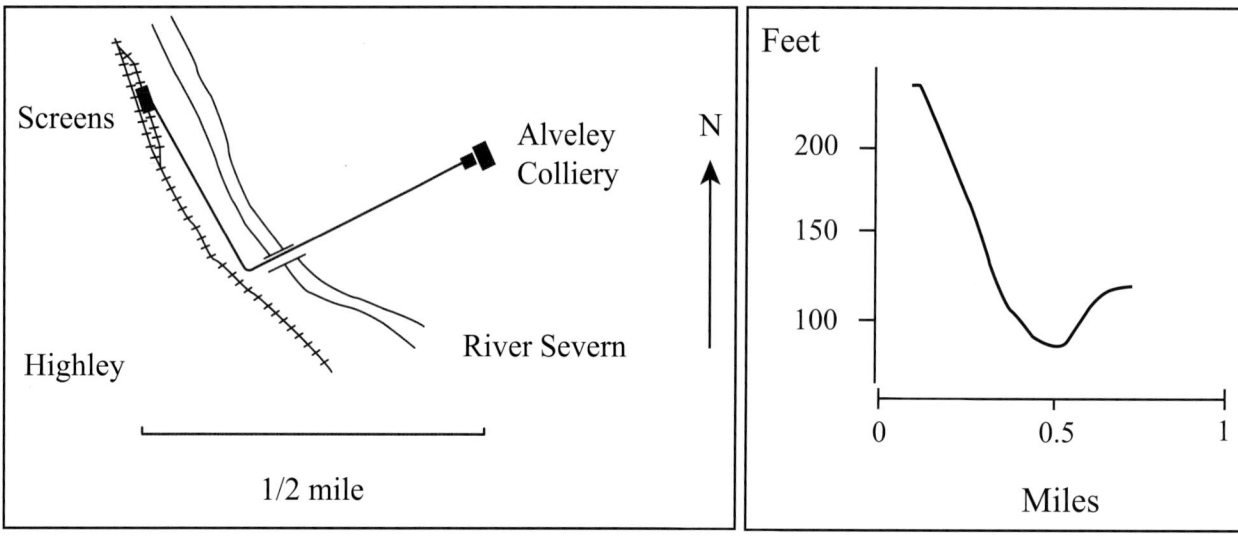

Figure 5.1a: Plan of the Alveley Colliery Ropeway.

Figure 5.1b: Alveley Colliery Ropeway Elevation.

In the mid-1950s, the National Coal Board decided to modernise Alveley, to access new reserves around three miles from the shaft. As part of this, it was decided to replace the surface tub haulage system. Initially three options were considered. The first was to replace the small tubs, each of which held 10cwt with large mine cars, holding 2 tons. These would run on a larger 2'3" gauge railway from the pit top to the screens and could be rope or locomotive-hauled. The other two options were to change the winding arrangements to skip winding (i.e. the coal was loaded underground into a large skip, which was wound up the shaft instead of a cage holding tubs). On the surface the coal would be discharged and taken to the screens either by conveyor or an aerial ropeway.[2] By the time the matter was discussed at the colliery modernisation committee on 1st December 1958, matters had moved forward.[3] It had been decided to use mine cars and locomotive haulage underground, with the mine cars being wound up the shaft. However, rather than take the mine cars all the way to the screens, the favoured scheme was now to return them underground as quickly as possible and go for the aerial ropeway option for onward movement of the coal. It was estimated that the ropeway would cost £160,568 but would require only 15 men instead of the 54 needed for the existing haulage. The final decision to build a ropeway was authorised on 3rd January 1959.[4]

As well as the ropeway and the underground haulage, it was necessary to deepen the shaft and carry out considerable remodelling of the colliery underground. The aim was to complete the works over the August bank holiday of 1960, allowing for a smooth changeover to the new systems. The contract for the ropeway was let to Mitchell's Ropeways of Doncaster, a company with much experience of working with the NCB. At the meeting of the colliery modernisation committee in June 1959 the NCB were hopeful that the ropeway would be ready by Whit Bank Holiday, June 6th, 1960. However at the August meeting the mood was darker. Mitchell's were asked for drawings of the ropeway as it was felt that it was unlikely to be completed by the August 1960 deadline. Ray Hasbury, the manager at Alveley, requested the use of the NCB mobile gang, as he did not have enough men to spare at Alveley to lay the ropeway out. The mobile gang, as their name suggested, were a group of craftsmen and labourers (led by Tom Weston from Granville Colliery) who worked at any construction project in the area that needed them. Help was forthcoming and a mix of Alveley Colliery employees and the mobile gang worked alongside specialised staff from Mitchell's. By March 1960 work was underway, with the construction of the angle station and preparatory work at the screens. The pylons were erected by early June and the ropeway was completed for the August changeover.[5]

The Alveley ropeway was 1175 yards long, turning through approximately 95° at an angle station a little beyond the Highley side of the bridge. Unlike other Shropshire systems, it used separate carrying and hauling ropes (Figure 5.2). The hauling rope was a conventional ¾" diameter wire rope. The carrying rope was a locked coil rope, 2.5" in diameter (Figure 5.3). Each of the 14 pylons had four steel girder legs, supported on concrete bases. The loading station was close to the pit top, next to the terminus of the former rope haulage system (Figure 5.4). Coal was brought to it by a short conveyor from the tippler, where the mine cars were emptied. Each bucket had a capacity of 2½ tons, the same as the mine cars used underground. There were originally 66 buckets. The buckets ran on four wheels whilst on shunt rails. Loading was fully mechanised, controlled by one man from a cabin that overlooked the loading point. The ropeway speed was 250 feet per minute and the capacity was reckoned at 200 tons of coal per hour or 50 tons of washery dirt. The 30hp driving motor for the ropeway was also at the loading system, as was the tensioning system for the driving rope. The latter was a conventional automatic system, relying on weights.[6]

Figure 5.2, left:
A close-up of a bucket close to the loading station on the ropeway, showing details of the dual-rope system, cradle and clip.

Figure 5.3, below:
The carrying (top) and driving (bottom) ropes used at Alveley. The driving rope is a Laing-pattern flattened-lay wire rope, designed to present a smooth surface to any pulley over which it would run. The rope is built around a central hemp core and would be very flexible. It is likely to be typical of the ropes used at other Shropshire ropeways. The carrying rope is of the locked coil design. The flattened wire strands on the outside of this rope give it a very smooth surface. It is made throughout of wire strands, making it strong but relatively inflexible.

Once loaded, the buckets ran along the ropeway and over the river, where the pylons were constructed immediately to the north of the bridge abutments (Figure 5.5). Where the ropeway ran over footpaths, shelters were constructed from steel rings (as used for underground roads) and concrete. A pair of guide wheels on the angle station redirected the ropeway to the screens (Figure 5.6). Here use was made of an existing discharge station built in the early 1950s (Figure 5.7). At that time, the final section of the tramway, where the tubs were taken up into the screens by a creeper and retarder, was replaced by a conveyor. The conveyor was kept, fed by a spiral chute from the discharge point. A pair of rails engaged with the sides of each bucket at this station and automatically opened a door in the bottom, allowing the coal to fall onto the chute. The buckets continued on their journey for a few more yards before entering the return station (Figure 5.8). Here a ramp and rails engaged with the door, hanging loosely from the bottom of the bucket and automatically closed it. The buckets passed

Figure 5.4: Loading and driving station at the colliery. **Note** the weights tensioning the rope; *see also Figure 1.3 on page 3.*

Figure 5.5: Ropeway pylons.

Figure 5.6: The ropway angle station.

26   SCMC Account 28 - Aerial Ropeways of Shropshire

Figure 5.7: Discharge station, Colliery screens. The early 1950s conveyor leads from the unloading station to the screens. The first buildings are the original screens built in 1939; behind is the washery, built in 1954.

round the shunt rail to return back to Alveley. However, before they were reattached to the rope, they were filled with slurry waste from the coal washery that treated the small coal (Figure 5.9). They then retraced their path back to the colliery, discharging the waste before being refilled. The waste was taken on the dirt conveyor to be emptied from the top of an elevator. It was then spread over the pit mound by a bulldozer.

The ropeway was not without its problems. The most serious of these became apparent immediately after opening. The carrying rope started to sag, so that the buckets approaching the bridge over the Severn dragged on the ground. The rope could not be tensioned sufficiently to solve the problem as the foundations of the return station were not robust enough to take the necessary strain. It was necessary to reinforce these with more concrete so a sufficiently high tension could be applied. A more minor problem came with the disposal of the slurry. This stuck to the sides of the first buckets that were used and they were eventually changed for another design that emptied easier. There were also problems from the weight of slurry; this could exceed the weight for which the buckets were designed and lead to slippages and collisions between buckets. In extreme cases this could lead to buckets coming off the ropes. This was a hazard of any ropeway. The heavy weight of the buckets used on the Alveley system, even when empty, made the problem of remounting them a difficult operation. Nonetheless, it is said that the ropeway paid for itself with a year of operation, in terms of labour saved. It ran without major incident until the colliery closed at the end of January 1969.[6]

The main surviving feature of the ropeway is the foundations of the angle station. Until recently, the piers for the pylons either side of the Alveley Colliery bridge also survived. However, the bridge has now been replaced and consequently the Highley pylon has been demolished. The entire Alveley pylon was buried under the embankment of the new bridge. At the visitor centre for the Severn Valley Country Park (on the mound of the former Alveley Colliery), a section of carrying rope is on display (Figure 5.3) and also a notice giving the signals code that was used to operate the ropeway (Figure 5.10). The latter was recovered from the screens.

SCMC Account 28 - Aerial Ropeways of Shropshire

Figure 5.8: Return Station, Colliery screens. **Note** the rails on the floor for automatically closing the door on the ropeway buckets.

Figure 5.9: Loading slurry at the return station.

Figure 5.10, below: Signal codes for the ropeway.

1. For a review, see R. Evans and D. Poyner, The Wyre Forest Coalfield, Tempus, Stroud, 2000, Chapter 5, pp 77-110.
2. Notes on Alveley modernisation, R. Evans Collection. These are not dated but belonged to the late R. Hemsley, chief surveyor at the colliery and were probably drawn up in early 1958.
3. Public Record Office COAL 77/5353
4. Public Record Office COAL 77/5353
5. Public Record Office COAL 77/5353
6. The information on the diameter of the carrying rope (based on field measurements) and the capacity of the buckets (oral information) differs from the records of Mitchell Ropeways, contained in a letter of 3-8-1978 to R. Evans. The carrying rope diameter was stated to be 2"diameter outgoing and 17/8" return, and the bucket capacity was 30cwt of coal, 78 cubic feet. Other information in this paragraph is from the Mitchell Ropeway letter.
7. Information from Messrs E. Edwards, R. Philpotts and G. Poyner, ex-Alveley Colliery employees.

6. Cosford Water Works

As urban populations increased water supply became a matter of concern with large conurbations looking to raid adjoining rural areas for supplies, Wolverhampton being no exception. The Wolverhampton New Waterworks Company built a plant at Cosford, just into Shropshire to extract water from River Worfe, it was completed in 1858 and taken over by Wolverhampton Corporation in 1867. Steam pumps were installed which required a constant supply of coal. It is not known what route was used initially to deliver coal, but one supposes that the railway must have been involved. Ruckley Siding SJ 7707 0641 was opened 19th July 1889 (Robinson 1980) for general goods, loam and coal for Cosford, which was worked forward by horse and cart, a process which did not please the highway authority. Around 1900 the Corporation proposed major works at Cosford included coal handling facilities. The initial scheme was for a tramway from a proposed siding on the main line to the works. This was planned in some detail and plans deposited for the necessary Act of Parliament. Before the end of 1902 the tramway idea had clearly been abandoned as by the 14th of February 1903, under the powers of the Local Government Provisional Order (No.18) of 1903, (to be known as The Wolverhampton Order 1903) the Corporation had signed a Memorandum of Agreement with the Hatton Grange Estate to purchase two pieces of land totalling 8 acres for ropeway and siding purposes and had been granted an easement for the ropeway to cross the intervening estate land in perpetuity subject to appropriate safeguards and conditions. A decision was made to have the Great Western Railway lay a different new siding and to build the ropeway from it to the works, the ropeway was to cost £4,000 to include fencing (Minutes 6th Dec 1905). The Corporation's Annual report of 9th November 1906 records that the use of Ruckley Siding ceased on 29th September 1906 and the use of Cosford Siding commenced 25th September 1906. It also reported that

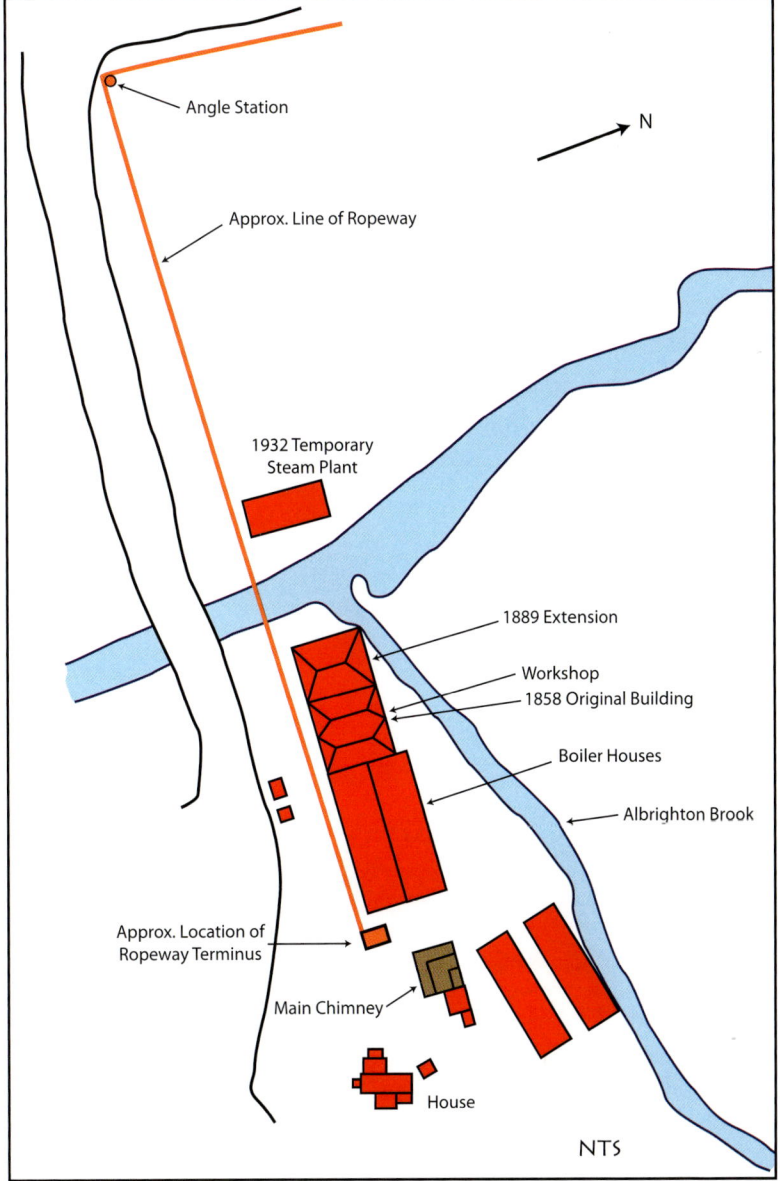

'The work of constructing the Aerial Ropeway and Railway Siding for dealing with the Coal traffic has been completed by Messrs. Ropeways, Limited, of London and the Great Western Railway Company, respectively. The new system of haulage was set in full operation on the 25th day of September, and is now working in a very satisfactory manner.'

Figure 6.1a:
Sketch plan of the works taken from the 1901 deposited plan with later information added.

SCMC Account 28 - Aerial Ropeways of Shropshire

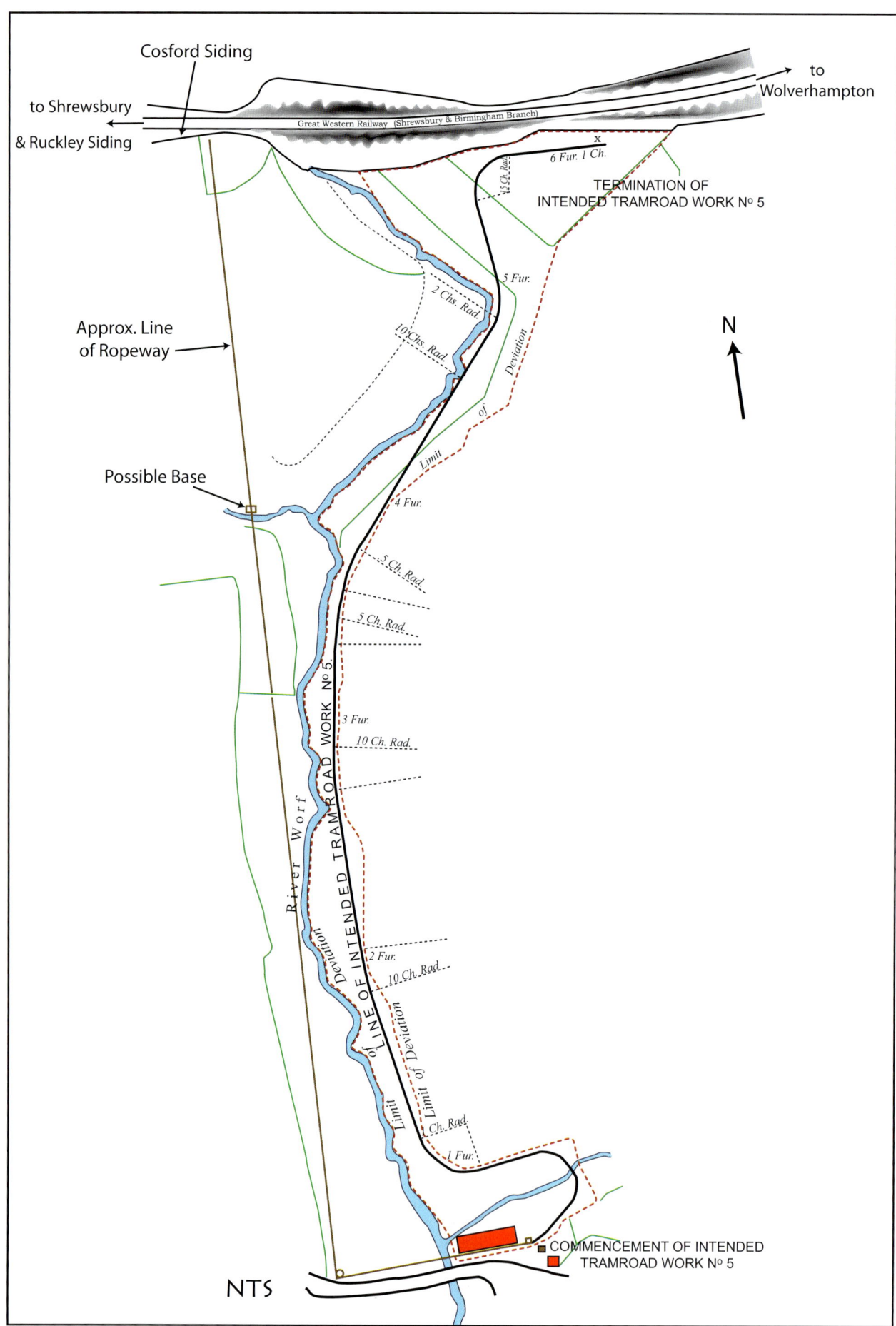

Figure 6.1b:
Sketch based on the 1901 deposited plan showing the proposed, but never build tramway, with the later ropeway and notes added.

The route of the ropeway differed from the proposed tramway, being to the west of the works rather than arriving at the rear from the east, the lie of the land being presumably the reason for that change. The ropeway line ran from a coal stage at the siding SJ 7813 0562 to an angle station by the road SJ 7796 0462 where it turned through about 90 degrees and initially ran past the front of the works to the powered return wheel cSJ 7810 0459 and the boiler house. This was modified c1932, see below.

There is no reason to doubt the performance of the ropeway but the performance of the boilers appears to have never been wholly satisfactory.[2] These were augmented with a temporary water tube boiler (to power a steam turbine) west of the works, near the line of the ropeway in 1922. By this time the works had eight steam pumping engines of various types, seven boilers, a steam generator set and two electrically driven pumps. A decision was made inter-alia to replace steam with mains electric pumping, under powers given by the Wolverhampton Corporation Act of 1932. Progress was slow due to keeping the works running and then was delayed by the war, the whole scheme was not finished until 1941. High tension mains and temporary electric pumps were installed in 1937 and the siding and ropeway ceased to function the following year when the siding agreement was terminated.[1] The ropeway was dismantled by August (see Figures 6.2 and 6.3).[2]

Figure 6.2:
The works from the West c1930s, with the temporary steam plant in the foreground and the ropeway passing towards the return wheel on the right. A rectangular 'bucket' is visible by what is presumably the coal hopper for that plant. The smoke from the main chimney makes it clear that some of the earlier boilers must have still been working.
(D Lloyd Collection)

Figure 6.3:
A similar photo to the above but the ropeway has gone and the temporary plant does not appear to be working, though a little smoke is coming from the main chimney.

The photograph is dated August 1938.
(D Lloyd Collection)

Figure 6.4:
The ropeway return wheel, the driving mechanism was in the shed below.

The house in the background still survives and the entrance to the new water works is approximately where the return wheel was.

(D Lloyd Collection)

Figure 6.5: Possible holding straps, April 2011. A third strap is visible at ground level at the end of white arrow. *(M Shaw)*

Figure 6.6: Possible bent remains of a pylon, April 2011. *(M Shaw)*

Figure 6.7: Detail of possible bent pylon remains, April 2011. *(M Shaw)*

The Remains

The remains are slight, 80 years of track maintenance have removed any trace of the siding, though a slight depression just visible in the cutting side opposite *could* be where the signal box was. There is a concrete or rendered masonry base with two protruding bolts just south of the site of the siding. This is presumably the remains of that end of the ropeway, though given that loam was dug around the site after the ropeway was removed one cannot be absolutely certain. A length of c40mm angle iron with what may be a brace bolted on are probably from the first pylon of the ropeway, though the previous proviso remains.

In the woods a little way south on an appropriate line c SJ 7820 5578 are three iron straps set into the ground which may be ropeway related. If they are, it suggests that rather than having concrete foundations with holding down bolts, as on many later lines, the pylons were anchored via these straps, this is rather speculative and could probable not be resolved for certain even by excavation.

In a hedge alongside the road from Tong (SJ 79172) to Shifnal is a length of multi-cored wire rope used as a fence. In the 1980s the rope ran from SJ 7917 0769 to SJ 7837 0779, a distance of almost ½ mile, although over the last few years, sections have been removed and the rope has deteriorated. This is only about a mile from the ropeway terminus at the railway sidings. Originally thought to have been a colliery winding rope, it is possible that it was used on the ropeway.

Figure 6.8: Base by the siding, April 2011.
(M Shaw)

Figure 6.9, above: Detail of part of the wire rope in the hedge near Tong. February 2009.
(K Lake - I.A.Recordings)

Figure 6.10: A section of the wire rope being used as a fence wire, in the hedge near Tong at SJ 7875 0769. February 2009.
(K Lake - I.A.Recordings)

Special Thanks

We would like to thank David Lloyd who at one time lived in the house in the background of Figure 6.4 (marked as Watermans Lodge on some maps) and whose father worked at the plant, for his assistance and for his permission to use his photographs (Figures 6.2, 6.3 and 6.4).

---

1. This was not the end of the use of the siding as loam was loaded from a 1924 extension westwards, this use had ceased by 1949 (Robinson 1980)
2. Anon, 'History of the Water Supply of Wolverhampton 1847-1947, Wolverhampton Corporation, 1947.

Other:
   Minutes of Wolverhampton Corporation.
   Robinson D H, 'The Wandering Worfe', Waine Research Publications, Wolverhampton, 1980.

7. Some Minor Ropeways

Whilst it is easy to document the main ropeways that worked in Shropshire, it is likely that there were also a significant number of smaller systems erected by contractors and others. By way of illustration, five of these will be described; they are surely representative of many more. Three are from the Highley area, where crossing the River Severn was always a problem.

The winter of 1895 was a particularly cold one and the Severn froze. This prevented the ferries from working. This was a blow for the Highley Mining Company. Whilst their order books must have been full to overflowing, around 50 of their miners living in Alveley were unable to get to work. Almost 20 years later, speaking at a meeting in favour of a bridge over the river, John Oakley Beddard, County Councillor for Highley recalled what happened next. The colliery manager (Thomas Bramley) "suspended an old pit rope between the two banks and the men hauled themselves across in a bucket".[1] Numerous ferries over the river at the time relied on working via a fixed rope between the banks (chain ferries) and it would not be surprising if these were also utilised for impromptu aerial ropeways when the ferries were unable to run.

Hampton Loade

At Hampton Loade, on the east bank of the river Severn, there had once been an iron forge (SO 747863). This stopped working in 1866 but demolition did not begin until 1890. One source states that the site was not cleared until 1900.[2] This may be true for the buildings, but a photograph said to date from 1906 shows ashes still being dug from the site (Figure 7.1).[3] These were said to be used for railway ballast. The photograph shows them being taken over the river by aerial ropeway. From the end of the ropeway, it is reported that the ashes were taken via a horse-operated tramway to Hampton Loade station.[4] The ropeway used separate carrying and driving ropes.

The picture suggests that the ropes were supported on wooden posts on either side of the bank. The driving rope appears to have been an endless rope powered by a horse gin on the west bank of the river. There seem to have been two wooden buckets, suspended by a pulley and chain from the clip that connected to the ropes. By hauling on the chain it was possible to raise and lower the buckets to the ground and detach them, for easier loading and unloading. Thus the ropeway resembled the "Blondins" used for moving stone from deep quarries.

Figure 7.1: Ropeway at Hampton Loade. The youth in the foreground is Edward Gwilt. **Note** the horse gin on the other side of the river, with Hampton Loade Station in the background.
(B. Cooper)

Alveley Colliery Bridge

As noted previously (Alveley Colliery Ropeway, Chapter 5 p22), in the mid 1930s the Highley Mining Company sank a new colliery in Alveley. To link this with the Severn Valley railway it was necessary to build a bridge with a 150' span over the Severn (SO 748 839). This was made of reinforced concrete and was designed by British Reinforced Concrete Ltd with Thomas Beighton of Macclesfield as contractors. Beighton's found it very difficult to access the Highley side of the river; the valley side is particularly steep here and the presence of the railway caused further problems. Accordingly, the Alveley bank was used as the main works site. Raw materials were brought to this by a temporary narrow-gauge tramway.

To transfer materials to the Highley bank, an aerial ropeway was built. This was a two cable system. The carrying rope was $7/_8$" diameter and was supported on wooden poles, being anchored to trees on each bank. The carrying rope was $3/_8$" diameter and was driven from one of the back wheels of an old an Austin 7 car which was anchored to the ground (Figure 11.2).

The principle traffic on the ropeway was concrete. This was mixed by machine and hoisted onto a truck running on rails mounted on a wooden gantry. The truck was pushed to the start of the ropeway, where the bucket was clipped to the rope to be hauled across the river. It took around 18 seconds for the 80 yard journey. At its peak, 400 runs a day were made over the ropeway and in total about 700 tons of concrete were carried.

Work started on the aerial ropeway on 30th June 1936, with the help of a temporary ferry. Construction of the bridge itself had begun by July 11th, but heavy rain and floods almost immediately brought work to halt; the river on July 15th was at a 50 year record high. The Austin 7 powering the ropeway had to be rapidly moved to higher ground. However, the floods soon subsided enough for work to start. On March 8th 1937 the main span was completed and it is likely that the ropeway was dismantled shortly afterwards. The entire contract passed without serious incident.[5]

Figure 7.2: The Austin 7 driving the ropeway at Alveley Colliery Bridge.

The car is mounted in concrete and the drive rope passes around the rear wheel.

(Collection of the Alveley Historical Society)

Snedshill Brickworks, Telford

Away from the Severn Valley, the Lilleshall Company installed what has been described as an "overhead bucket conveyor" at Snedshill Brickworks (SJ 700 102) to take clay from a claypit to the stock yard, in the years before the First World War.

It appears to have been commissioned by J.H. Baxendale, the brickyard manager who oversaw the modernisation of the works. This is probably the same as the aerial ropeway which operated between the Hydraulic Pit (SJ 701 109) and the brickworks from c1914 to c1920. The Hydraulic Pit was just under ½ a mile north of the brickworks; it had closed some time before the ropeway was built, but the clay from the mound was used for the bricks. Unfortunately no further details are currently available about this system.[6]

Doseley Quarry, Dawley

What may have been another aerial ropeway was in operation at Doseley Quarry (SJ 675 067), near Dawley, in the late 1920s. Doseley was a basalt quarry, operated after the First World War by Messrs Johnson Brothers, in conjunction with a brick works. The quarry was visited in 1929 by members of the Shropshire Surveyors Association. The overburden at the quarry was removed by steam shovel to expose the rock. Some of this consisted of clay and was taken by light railway to the brick works. The rest was "deposited by special hoisting machinery on to a spoil tip". The "special hoisting machinery" may be an aerial ropeway. It must have been very short, presumably running from a screening plant to the spoil tips.

---

1 Kidderminster Times, 9-5-14
2 N. Mutton, The forges at Eardington and Hampton Loade, Trans. Shrop. Arch. Soc., 56, 1966, Pg 243.
3 Collection of Mr W. Cooper, Romsley
4 J. Tennant, The Billingsley and Kinlet Railways, Severn Valley News, Autumn 1974, 24, Pg 26
5 A.P. Mason, Alveley Bridge, Concrete and Constructional Engineering, August 1937, Pp 453-9.
6 W.K.V. Gale and C.R.Nicholls, The Lilleshall Company; a history 1764-1964, Moorland Publishing, Ashbourne, 1979, Pg 65; I.J. Brown, News Round-Up, Below 2000:2 Pg 2; Special Report on Mineral Resources of Great Britain, Volumes 14, Refractory materials; fireclays, resources and geology, HMSO, 1920, Pg 149.
7 Anon, The Surveyor, Vol 76, 1929, Pg 61

Part 2: West Shropshire

The Stiperstones' Ropeways - Introduction

After excess water perhaps the most common cause of the failure of a decent mine has been transport. Barytes being both dense and produced in quantity has created its share of problems though substantial production levels did not build up until the 20th century when the transport options had expanded somewhat. Five barytes mines and one stone quarry in south west Shropshire opted for air transport, using ropeways. Technological developments in the later 19th century led to the development of small diameter wire ropes with a good carrying capacity which enabled the aerial ropeway to become viable. Initially used in Scottish granite quarries more as cranes than transport they soon spread and enjoyed a vogue from before the First World War until the 1960s. One, at a brickworks at Claughton near Lancaster still runs but is was said to be due for replacement using ski lift technology.

The lines described in the next chapters all used a single rope which provided both load bearing and traction. The rope was wound from a motor at one end. The buckets had an arm with a bracket which rested on the rope via a grooved shoe, the groove being just less than the diameter of the rope, and as the rope moved gravity held the buckets and they moved with it. It does not need a vivid imagination to see that on steep slopes, wet, oily or icy rope or with high winds swinging the bucket (and they don't need any wind at all to swing them, they do it all the time) 'deropements' would occur. It is probable that the short life of the Perkins Beach line was due to the fearsome gradient up to Beach Hill and there are memories of bucket after bucket on the main line from Bog crashing down from that hill to form a heap behind Stiperstones school.

> 'There was a very steep part above the Stiperstones where it came straight over the hill and many a time a bucket would slip and you would hear 'em coming bang, bang, bang.'[1]

The buckets were also equipped with double flanged wheels which would run on the monorail shunt rails provided at junctions and termini. Power could be provided by steam, diesel or electricity, Bog and Huglith used electricity and Perkins Beach (portable) steam, it is not known what power was used for the Buxton Quarry line, probably portable steam, possibly diesel.

Steel trestles were presumably prefabricated locally and Atlas Foundry have been mentioned as a possible supplier. Unfortunately no photographs of the steel trestles on the Bog line have surfaced though all the in-situ bases noted have been for triangular ones, one photograph shows a triangular one at Huglith. On lines elsewhere and therefore probably in Shropshire, these have generally been constructed of smallish angle, often 2 inch (50 mm), with circular section bar braces triangulating them (as the Huglith one seems to be). Where four legged steel trestles have been noted they seem to often have been entirely made of angle iron, though local evidence is totally lacking. Specific information for the Bog line and on non-standard structures is to be found below.

Sketch of a Huglith ropeway pylon, 1949.
(M Newton)

---

1 Mollie Rowson (born 1908) remembering her school days in 'Never on a Sunday', Shropshire Mines Trust, 2000

8. The Bog Line and Branches

By the early twentieth century Bog mine had had a long history as a reasonably good lead mine which produced some barytes, zinc and a little silver. It had operated at least from the late seventeenth century but had closed and reopened several times in the nineteenth. A significant reopening occurred in 1910 when Shropshire Lead Mines Ltd. began an investment campaign with barytes as the principal aim. Ramsden's Shaft was sunk and a large amount of plant including a gas producer and electricity generator installed. The first of the ropeways discussed below represents the last phase of this campaign. Perkins Beach contained a series of small mines from about the 1840s, these enjoyed a similar stop start existence to Bog, sometimes under the same management. Wotherton Barytes and Lead Mining Co Ltd. took on some leases just before the First World War and did some development at the lower end of the valley (known as Perkins Beach Mine) and at the upper end of the valley (as New Venture Mine). Shropshire Lead Mines Ltd. amalgamated with the Wotherton company in 1916 to form Shropshire Mines Ltd. who did further development at Bog and Perkins Beach including the ropeways. Buxton Quarry, which also had a ropeway branch seems to have been developed after the war and had ceased producing by the mid 1920s.

A mine with a direct rail connection, such as Snailbeach, was quite well off for transport but go a few miles from their railhead to Bog mine and matters were quite different. Whether it was the cost of the extra handling at Crowsnest or the unreliability or the charges of the Snailbeach District Railway (SDR), Shropshire Lead Mines Ltd. and their successors, Shropshire Mines Ltd. chose to haul at least some of their barytes direct to Minsterley station using traction engines and trailers. This wrecked the roads and the local authorities had copious correspondence with them (as well as a number of other mines) on that subject. The matter was settled to some extent by contributions in cash or by the mine companies maintaining the roads in good repair. The County Council were responsible for the main road from Plox Green to Minsterley and Chirbury Rural District Council for the minor roads onwards to the mine.[1] The First World War exacerbated matters with extra production required by HMG and work-force shortages, no doubt road maintenance was a matter the mine would have been happy to do without. On 23 March 1916 the Chirbury RDC correspondence revealed that the mine was considering either an aerial transport system or a tramway along the road to Pennerley and Bog.

A further factor in the transport needs was fuel, around 1914 a gas powered generator had been built at Bog and needed considerable quantities of coal, some (most?) of which had come so far on the SDR, having been trans-shipped 'uphill' at Pontesbury junction, and finished its journey, also against the gradient, by road. Correspondence surviving from 1916 and 1917 between the Snailbeach District Railway and Shropshire Lead Mines makes it clear that there were problems. Bog mine was forecasting 1,300 tonnes a month outward traffic in March 1916 (which was never remotely approached). Eighteen months later, a few days after they were notified of a rise in the railway charges, the mine company were complaining that they were waiting for trucks.

> '200 tons now waiting rail and over 100 tons of this quantity is...at the Rwy Sidings at Snailbeach awaiting shipment to Pontesbury...'[2]

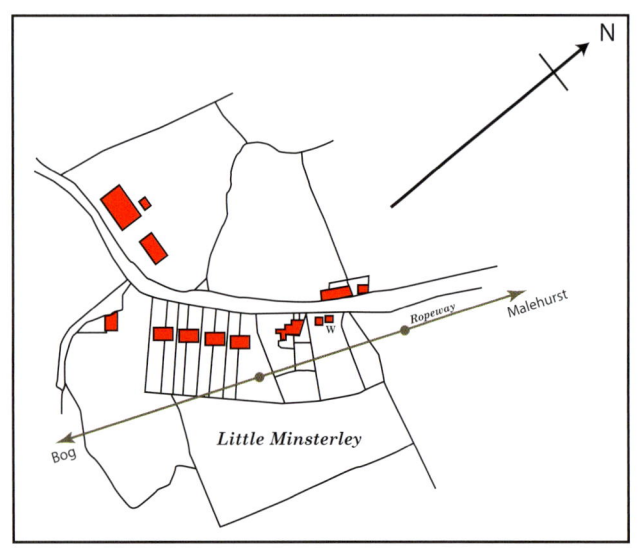

Figure 8.1:
Sketch map based on the deeds of numbers 9 and 10 Little Minsterley, showing the line of the aerial ropeway across the fields behind the houses.
Note: The trestle positions shown do not actually tie up with what little was found on site during a field walking session in 2003.

('On the High Road', Francis P, private, Shrewsbury, 2001)

Figure 8.2:
A view down the Buxton Quarry line from near the Transfer Station. Note the lack of vegetation round the base and the telephone line insulators.
(Emily Griffiths Collection)

The tramway considered above would have effectively been a re-jigging of one of the un-built proposals to extend the Snailbeach railway and would have suffered from the same problems, i.e. how to get past Mytton Dingle, Perkins Beach and the smaller dingles, economically.[3] The lie of the land precluded a road-side line and it would not have removed the trans-shipment problem unless it had been actually or effectively an extension of the Snailbeach Railway. The ropeway equally could not have followed the road but it did finally run loosely parallel to it.

Ropeways Limited no doubt supplied and erected the line as their Chief Engineer's (John Roe) monocable system and patent process for changing direction were used. At the time of construction the Electrical Journal stated that it was the longest ropeway yet built in the UK.

Figure 8.3:
Front of a 1920s Ropeways business card. *(Claughton Brickworks)*

The Main Line

Insufficient information has yet come to light to allow a definite chronology of the ropeways but from the known facts a good skeleton can be assembled. The earliest clear action towards the ropeway was the purchase of the houses numbers one to twelve, Little Minsterley in September 1917. This enabled Shropshire Mines Limited to build and access the ropeway across the gardens (figure 8.1), but it may also have indicated that they were involved in major investment in the Minsterley area, though it was to be 1925 before Malehurst Mill came on stream by which time the houses had been resold. The necessary clause to permit access to the ropeway was included when the houses were sold in 1922 and 1923 and in at least one case was still enforceable in 1934.[4]

A lease for the ropeway to cross fields for about two thirds of a mile (about 1 km) between Stiperstones and Snailbeach was granted by the Lloyd Estate (figure 8.4). It was to be valid from 30 June 1918, though it was not signed until 1920. It stipulated that the ropeway was to be built within two years, there were to be no more than eight trestles (sometimes known locally as trussels, and sometimes pylons, standards or towers) of timber or steel each to be not more than fifteen feet square with ten feet clearance to the rope over fields and fifteen feet over roads. The trestles were to be as near the hedges as possible. The lease covered all minerals from the mine and from any mine belonging to the lessees. It was for 21 years at £26 p.a. rent. On termination of

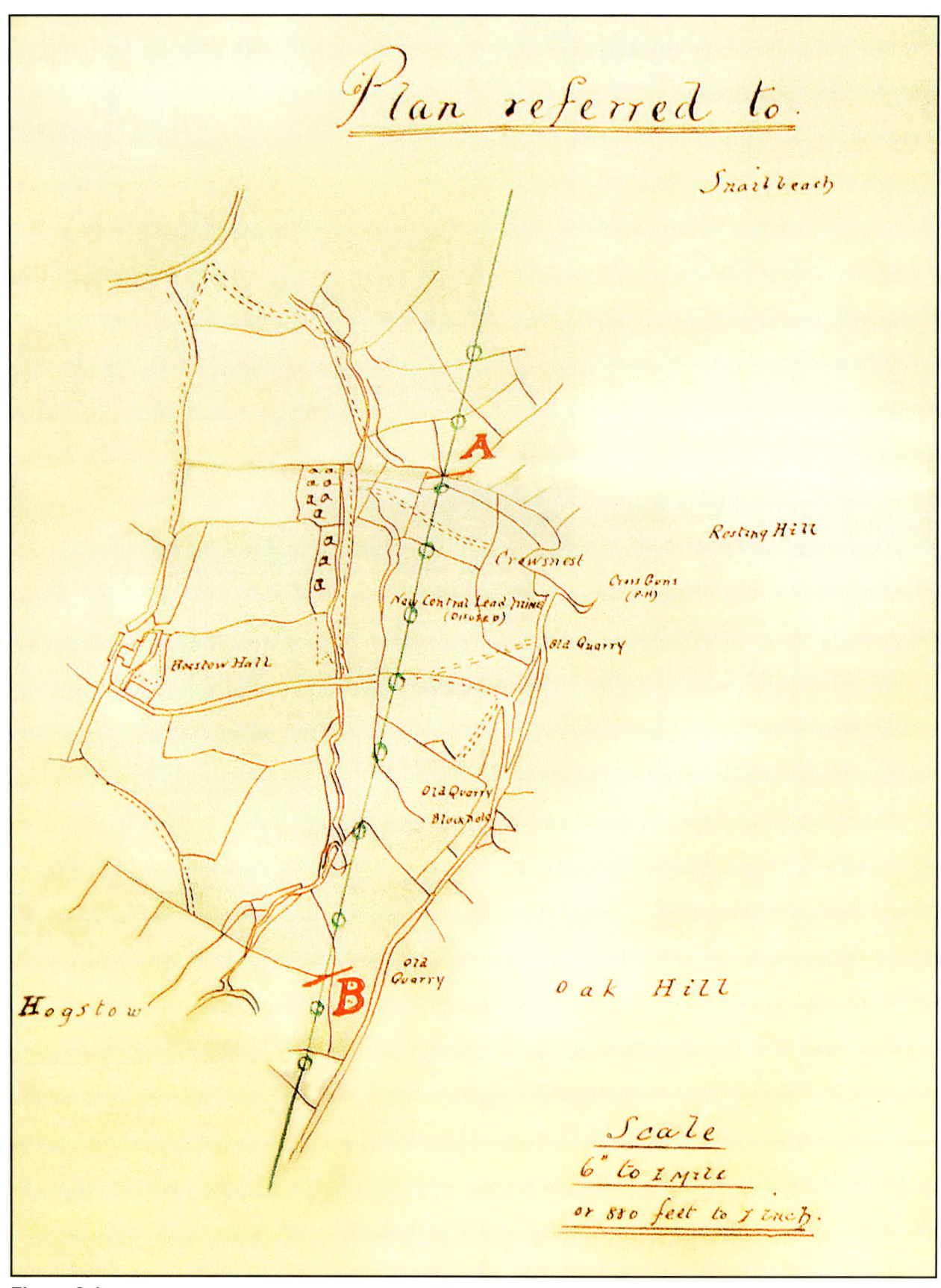

Figure 8.4:
The Lloyd Estate agreement plan drawn up to allow the ropeway to cross fields for about two thirds of a mile (approximately 1 km) between Stiperstones and Snailbeach.

(Shropshire Archives SA4929 3 2)

Figure 8.5:
The 'Institute' (aka The Cabin) at Bog Mine (in 1980 shortly before it was demolished), where it is said by some the German POWs were housed during the construction of the ropeway.
(K Lake - I.A.Recordings)

the lease the land was to be reinstated within six months. If Bog Mine was not worked for twelve months the lessor could remove the ropeway.[5]

Other evidence points clearly to construction taking place during 1918. It was still under construction in the November as locals remember the German prisoners of war, involved in its construction celebrating the armistice. Initially the Germans were housed in the Midland Railway yard at Coleham, Shrewsbury and marched to work daily from Minsterley station. Later they occupied the 'Institute' (aka The Cabin) at Bog Mine (figure 8.5), the walls of which now house tourist interpretation boards. Henry Jones of Pennerley remembers his grandmother telling him that they also used her shed for accommodation and she supplemented their rations, in return they would tip ropeway buckets of coal out as they passed her house. The locals remember them with affection and as good craftsmen. When the ropeway actually opened is unknown but Mollie Rowson (born in 1908) remembers being taken out of school to see the first bucket go down the line.[6]

Legalities are also recorded from 1918. An agreement was entered with the County Council for the line to cross the main road at Poulton on 19th October 1918.[7] That Shropshire Mines Ltd. owned the site at Malehurst is not in doubt as it is specified in the Lloyd lease above, but what was there in 1918 is not known, the mill was not built until 1924/1925. An agreement is recorded in the GWR Register of Private Sidings for Malehurst in the name of the Malehurst Barytes Co. Ltd, this notes that the original agreement was dated 23rd July 1919,[8]

Figure 8.6:
The transfer station on Beach Hill, junction with the Buxton branch. To the left the main line continues to Bog Mine, right to Minsterley. The Buxton branch drops off the edge of the platform into the valley.
(Emily Griffiths Collection)

Figure 8.7:
The ropeway transfer station, the Buxton branch is off to the left, c1920. The main line rope from the Bog passes overhead and drops under the rails and frame to the right. *(Emily Griffiths Collection)*

and a siding is known to have been in use in 1921. Assuming that it is correct that both ropeways used the same unloading facility, and as this seems to have always been some distance from the railway, quite a substantial siding would have been needed to serve it.

At some early stage, possibly from the start, a branch line ropeway served Perkins Beach mine(s), it probably closed before 1920 clearly not having been successful. By late 1919 Shropshire Mines were developing Buxton Quarry for roadstone and hoped to have a ropeway branch to serve it by April 1920 (see below). Like the Perkins Beach line it met the main line at the junction station (locally and perhaps officially called the transfer station) on Beach Hill, but it is not clear (and local opinion will give you all possible answers) whether the junction was built with the main line or inserted into it after that line was constructed. Various possibilities emerge:

1. That the Perkins Beach branch was built at the same time as the main line.
2. That the Buxton branch was also planned and a four way junction installed.
3. That the junction was inserted after the construction of the main line for one or both branches.
4. That the junction, whenever it was installed, was reconstructed after the closure of Perkins Beach line to accommodate the Buxton line.

It does not seem likely that the company would have gone to the trouble of inserting a junction station after the main line was finished, this would have involved some interesting threading of ropes. From the surviving photographs with the Buxton branch extant it seems that a branch line needed its own projecting structure (which is not visible in figure 8.6 on the Perkins Beach side of the junction). I therefore suggest that the most likely scenario is that the main and Perkins Beach lines were constructed together and after the failure of the branch the junction was re-jigged to serve Buxton Quarry. The photograph of the Buxton line working (figures 8.2, 8.6 and 8.7) must be early on in its life as there is very little sag in the loaded line and no weeds round the bases. The photographs at the junction station are also probably from when it was new (possibly the same day), everything looks very trim and there are what may be building materials and tools around the site. There is no sign of the line from Perkins Beach.

The line from Bog ran until the closure of that mine in mid October 1925 and by that time Buxton Quarry had also ceased using it. The County Council's records come to our aid next, it was reported to the Roads and Bridges Committee on 26th January 1926 that Shropshire Mines Limited were in liquidation and that both ropeways (Bog and Huglith) were considered abandoned, the committee resolved as follows:

1. 'That the council be recommended to affix their common seal to a deed conditionally assigning to the Malehurst Barytes Coy Ltd. the licence granted to the Shropshire Mines Ltd. dated 23rd July 1921'.
2. 'That the clerk and County surveyor be authorised to dispose of the Bog mine Ropeway'.[9]

To what extent the clerk and County surveyor actually acted is not known but the line was dismantled probably in 1927. Some of the equipment was exported to Santander in northern Spain for reuse, this seems not particularly surprising as there was much British investment in the area prior to the Spanish Civil War and an office of Ropeways Ltd. It is also said that the rope was wound onto two drums and stored for some time in a field near Stiperstones school which were finally removed by a traction engine which caught fire somewhere en route to Snailbeach.[10]

The strength and weakness of a ropeway is that it must go in more or less straight lines (but see below) and whilst these are the shortest routes no allowance can be made for obstructions. The Bog line went straight over Beach Hill to a point halfway between Snailbeach and Wagbeach where it turned through a few degrees to carry on to Malehurst. Plotting an entirely straight route indicates problems. It would have started by having to go over the Bog school roof which would have involved not only unjustified risks from falling material but two substantial trestles to gain and maintain height. It would then have had to span Perkins Beach and Mytton Dingle in one go at a considerable height and possibly have trestles on the sides of steep hills with the cross fall giving a consequent increase in the problems of construction, stability and maintenance. It would also have almost followed the road through parts of Perkins Beach, Crowsnest and Snailbeach, not the ideal locations given the propensity for the buckets to drop off or shed their loads.

The line began at a loading point near the eastern edge of the Bog mine site, on the south of the track to Ritton. It then passed behind the school - the iron fence behind the school yard no doubt dates from this period, it was to stop the children playing underneath the rope. It then crossed the road and headed over the upper slopes of Pennerley and the top end of Tankerville Dingle to the junction station on Beach Hill. Here, as set out above the two branches came in. There was some sort of building just below the ropeway, no doubt for the men (actually two boys) who were employed there moving buckets on and off the branch lines.[11] From here it passed so near the ground that a cutting had to be dug to clear the buckets. The line then dropped off the hill in its longest single span of about a quarter of a mile (390m on the map) to an 80 foot (85 according to some)(about 25m) high steel trestle in the field behind Stiperstones school. It ran along the valley between Hogstow Hall and Central Snailbeach, passed over where Snailbeach football ground now is and changed direction. It then crossed Farm Lane, the site of Minsterley football ground, the rear of Little Minsterley's houses and crossed the main road at Poulton where there were bins at the roadside for the stone from Buxton. The road crossing was protected from falling buckets and their contents by a safety net though the later Huglith line had a proper steel bridge. After passing across fields it arrived at Malehurst.

The ropeway terminus at Bog Mine was at the lower end of the rope worked tramway from Ramsden's Shaft[12] where barytes was tipped from the high level line into a wooden hopper which was either wholly or mostly surrounded by the return rails for the ropeway. The rope passed round a vertical sheave in each direction, the (presumably) underground layout of the rope, motor and tensioner cannot be deduced from the only known photograph but it no doubt involved a horizontal sheave in a chamber below the terminus framework or at the lower ground level to the north of it, the motor could possibly have been at the same location or in the adjoining building.

Lubrication was by drip feed from a tank at the driven end. The electric motor was a 60hp, 3 phase, 500v, 726 rpm, 625 amperes, 25h.p., which was sufficient to operate the line when a full load was carried downhill. Initially it powered the line at 100 yards per minute but it was planned to increase this to 120 yards per minute.

At first only half the intended number of buckets were provided, unfortunately we do not know how many that was, but as buckets numbered 100 and 101 appear in a photograph (figure 8.8) we know something. It is doubtful if the full number were ever provided, one local source suggests that there were 127. Quite where the anthracite that was brought up the line was discharged is not known, though the Royal Engineers Journal[13] contains the following informative note:

> 'Intermediate Unloading Station—For unloading anthracite on the return journey. Requires no detailed description.'

Figure 8.8:
A photograph of the Bog ropeway terminus from before 1922. The high level tramway from Ramsden's shaft is visible discharging into the wooden hopper.

(The Electrical Journal, Volume 86, Dec 31st 1921, Pg 36)

Figure 8.9:
Remains of the ropeway terminus at the Bog Mine, 5th May 1970.
(G L Jones, Shropshire Photographic Society)

The Trestles

The same journal states that most trestles were of steel, though site investigation shows that to be unlikely, though there were steel ones in critical locations. Steel ones are known from remains to have been at the road crossing by Bog School, behind Stiperstones school and behind number seven Little Minsterley and at the main road crossing at Poulton and possibly at the other road crossings (though not at Callow lane where the bases for a wooden one survive). By implication there were steel trestles at the Stiperstones inn and Farm Lane crossings.[14] The steel ones were constructed from angle 'compressed to 60 degrees' where horizontal braces were fitted, and were three legged. They were erected bolted together in 2m stages on a concrete base for each leg.

Wooden trestles consisted of four poles, to judge from surviving evidence eight to ten inches (200-250mm) in diameter (the timber is remembered as being cut at Crowsnest). The poles were set on a foundation, described as 'a massive block of concrete'[15] which at a guess would have been about two foot thick (600 mm) and down to bedrock or at least firm natural ground. As no reports of collapses or capsizes are known, given the degree that the buckets could swing, the foundations must have been well done. On this base the poles were set up and presumably at this stage bolted at the top and braced. When all was well, shuttering would have been placed round the foot of each pole and a concrete pad poured to give some lateral stability. There is evidence that the pads were rendered on their upper surfaces to reduce the ingress of water it is also possible that they, and the wooden trestles were painted. These pads are the most numerous survivors both in and ex situ.

The trestles were fitted with running gear which consisted of sets of pivoted jockey wheels over which the rope ran with enough clearance for the bucket brackets to pass over. Normally one pair of wheels were sufficient for each direction. However, where changes in gradient were greater, two sets of pairs of wheels were provided for the loaded direction (the side heading towards Minsterley), or sometimes, both directions.

The trestles were numbered on plates about eight inches long, though none are visible on photographs. One local thinks that the trestle at the bottom of the cutting on Beach Hill was number 20 and one on top of Pennerley 22 or 27. If that is the case there are not enough numbers for them to have been numbered from Malehurst. Number 20 at the bottom of the cutting 2km from Bog ties up with the numbering commencing there as generally the spacing of trestles seems to have been about 100m, though this leaves 22 or 27 impossible. The trestles also boasted ladders on their upper reaches to assist with the periodical greasing and maintenance.

Steel trestles are neither so well documented nor represented by remains. One bolt (B02 on Map 1, page 65) projected out of the grass verge by Bog School until recently though now it has gone, presumably buried. Behind Stiperstones School the size of the base is still apparent but the unsuccessful post war attempt to blow it up has left it somewhat difficult to interpret. Of the base behind number seven Little Minsterley one bolt still projects from its tall (about 600mm) foundation, on the assumption that it was a triangular trestle the other two bases could survive under shrubbery in the adjoining garden. No photographs of a steel trestle are known. There may not have been a standard steel trestle, if there was the Little Minsterley one may be an example. Judging from a postcard (figure 8.10) the base by Bog School, photographed after the removal of the trestle, had six foundations, it is believed that this was where the coal was offloaded, so would have needed additional supports. The Stiperstones school trestle was clearly a special case. Until the late discovery of additional information[16] it was assumed that there was an angle station near Snailbeach for the route to diverge a few degrees, however this divergence was taken up over a length of 0.823km in eight spans using Roe's patent (128650 of 1917) in a method described in the Royal Engineers Journal[17] as follows:

> "On the trestles in the curve the sheaves are mounted as usual on balance beams. The balance beam carrying the sheaves is suspended on a laterally swinging arm which permits the beam and sheaves to swing outwards or inwards from the standard while the load passes, and this obviates any tendency for the rope to mount the flanges of the sheaves owing to change of direction. The wear on the sheaves is admitted to be slightly increased owing to the curve, but it is not great."

The actual divergence is stated to have been 7 degrees over 7 trestles, from the base at B44 past B48 (our numbering scheme), see the table in Appendix A amd Map 1 (pages 64 and 65).

Near where there was initially thought to have been an angle station there is a 'tip' containing seven pads for wooden poles, three tall bases for (presumably) one steel trestle and two blocks of concrete with lengths of angle iron projecting. Quite what these latter were actually for is moot, unless the bases on the turn needed some addition lateral restraint, either when erected or after a period of use. These remains are partly in the stream, partly buried, somewhat overgrown and tell very little.

There were 75 trestles stated to be at 98 yard spacing, though this does not make up the 5.5 miles, maybe 98 yards is the most common spacing, coming down from Beach Hill to the field behind the school there was a much longer span.

Figure 8.10:
R.M. & S. Ltd. postcard with 5 views around Bog including one of the school (right) showing five of the six bases, the sixth (arrowed) is just in the edge of the road. The card was produced after 1927 and before 1940 as a copy of the card exists with a 1940 postmark.

The Rope

The main line rope was an impressive 11 miles (17.5 km) long, it arrived on drums in several lengths the largest of which weighed 7 tonnes. It would have been wound off the drums directly onto the trestles and then spliced at seven points. Splicing was an expert job, each splice would have been 40 feet (12m) long and been carried out during installation, when the rope broke or when it stretched so far that the tensioning system could no longer cope, (at another Shropshire ropeway this was an extension of 75 feet (22.5m)). The tensioning was done at the mine using a 4 tonne concrete block through a 4 to 1 system giving an effective load of 16 tonnes, the precise location and layout of this are not clear.

The rope was a stranded Langs lay, 'three and one eighth inch' in circumference (about 24mm diameter). The branches would have had separate ropes, if they did not exist at the same time it is possible that the Perkins Beach rope could have had an extra 550 yards (500 m) spliced on to work to Buxton or that the terminus at that quarry was not where we think, but was somewhat short thus enabling the same, unaltered rope to be reused.

The junction station was complex and despite having two reasonable photographs of it, its modus operandi is obscure. Buckets to or from a branch had to pass over one direction of the main rope, which was lowered (see figure 8.6) and buckets on both the main line and branch had to use the rails. There may have been some sort of moveable blade switch on the shunt rails. It is possible that buckets had to be manually reversed in each direction for either branch or that full buckets may have used the 'empties' line to Bog mine and then returned for a second time to pass the junction, with empties doing the reverse. The fact that the Perkins Beach line came in 'against the flow' will not have helped.

At Malehurst where the ropeway terminated (with the usual sheave and rails) there was initially a steel framed structure with a hopper below for barytes and a raised hopper for anthracite in each case to facility loading into or unloading from main line railway wagons. Later, following the construction of Malehurst Mill (completed a few months before the closure of Bog Mine, see figure 9.4 in the next chapter) a new or much altered hoist was constructed to take the barytes up to second floor level where it passed downwards through the various process stages. When only the Bog line was working the telephone system carried on the trestles would have been used to start and stop the rope and to switch between the branch and the main line, once the Huglith line opened it would have been included in this system. A bell system activated by the rope was installed at Bog but the men preferred to use their eyes when spacing the buckets.

The remains are not always easy to find and are of course somewhat spread out. The data list in Appendix A (page 64) gives locations of the ones found (mainly) during the summer of 2003 (or Summer 2004 for the Huglith line) with grid references, these are all marked on the maps in the appendix, but not commented on. Not all of these sites are on public footpaths and permisison from the landowners to view them must be obtained. There are probably other remains in situ which have not been looked for, but these will probably add no new knowledge and enough has been recorded to be precise about the alignments.

The concrete foundations and holding down bolts of much of the Bog terminus are visible. Over the top to Beach Hill there are several sets of pads for wooden trestles visible including two dumped off line by a reservoir. The transfer station has one of the best sets of remains. The entire site has been levelled from the hillside and at ground level there are a series of concrete foundations and bolts and as a bonus there is a full set of four pads for a trestle on the Buxton branch and an odd ex situ base. Across the hillside from here are bases at the top and bottom of the cutting on the main line and a view down the line toward Stiperstones School. The exploded remains of the big trestle base here lie jumbled in the field with a base for a strut or stay in the next field. Odd sets of bases lie about the fields and hedges. The eye of faith is totally strained at Malehurst itself.

Each bucket could carry 5 hundredweight (0.25 ish of a tonne) of barytes, about 4.5 of stone and rather less of anthracite. The capacity of the line was a total of 20 tonnes of barytes and 5 tonnes of anthracite an hour and potentially 38,000 tonnes a year at a cost of about 2d (~1p) a tonne-mile compared with the previous cost of around 3/- (15p) a tonne-mile.

The ropeway cannot ever have carried a great deal. In 1916 the mine, (including Nipstone, Nipstone Rock and Nipstone Bog) was producing 7,046 tonnes which, had they had a ropeway working 300 days a year it would have carried 23.5 tonnes per day i.e. 94 bucket loads. By 1918 with the ropeway possibly in use very late in the year, production was down to 3,260 tonnes, by the same criteria eleven tonnes or 44 buckets per day. Figures thereafter do not survive but the number employed fell gradually, so no doubt did production and use of the ropeway. There is no memory of how the line was run, it is possible that barytes was stockpiled at the mine until a days running was ready, though the Huglith line is known to have run twice a day to a timetable. Traffic from Bog had of course to share the line with that from Perkins Beach or Buxton.

After dismantling, the steel will have been reused or recycled and the timber used for fence posts, sheds, firewood etc. Henry Jones used to have a shed built of timber from the trestles (and thought he might still have a number plate from one, though he hasn't found it). The trestle's fixed ladders were also recycled locally, in one case Wilson Morgan and Mr Rowson roofed a dairy using one inside and then found that it was too large to get it out.

The Perkins Beach branch

A short steep ropeway rising about 415 feet (125m) in the first 900 feet (270m) of its run from Tabertail. An undated plan of the valley, which shows the main line, refers to the branch in a note, it implies 1919/1920 for a date and that it was worked by a portable steam engine, which no doubt did its own tensioning.

That the line had gone by December 1919 is suggested by a reference in a Christmas newsletter to Shropshire Mines staff. This informed them that amongst the improvements to be made was the ropeway to Buxton Quarry and a light railway to connect Perkins Beach Mine near Tabertail to the ropeway. While it cannot be definitely established it is not likely that the railway would have been from elsewhere in the valley to Tabertail, but is much more likely to be a railway from Tabertail to the field behind Stiperstones school replacing the branch ropeway, the railway was never built. The only information about the ropeway line is that there was said to be a 90 foot (27m) high trestle in the valley. The base of this may remain but has not been found. There is a possible site of a trestle base on the flank of Beach Hill (see the data list in Appendix A, page 68) and the remains of a concrete pad at the site of the possible terminus (see pictures on page 61).

SCMC Account 28 - Aerial Ropeways of Shropshire

The Buxton Quarry branch

The first two wooden trestle bases from the junction station are the only known remains of this line. A trestle is remembered at Flagpole corner but this will have gone due to road improvements. It is not clear where at the quarry it terminated, it could have been almost on Tankerville Mine tips and could possibly have been used from there as well. It is also not known how it was powered though a portable steam engine (possibly the one from Perkins Beach) is not an unreasonable suggestion.

Figure 8.11:
Workers believed to have been engaged in erecting the aerial ropeway near Roundhill Mine on the Buxton Quarry branch, c1920.
Back row, left to right: R.Rowson, J.G.Williams, G.Williams, unknown, T.Hill.
Front row, left to right: unknown, S.Purslow, J.Purslow, R.Purslow, T.Lewis.

(K.C.Lock)

Figure 8.12:
The four concrete pads for timber trestle posts on the Buxton Quarry branch, by the transfer station on Beach Hill, 26 May 2004.

(Q01 on Map 1, page 65 and Map 3, page 68).

(M Shaw)

48　　　　　　　　　　　　　　　　　　　　　　　　　　SCMC Account 28 - Aerial Ropeways of Shropshire

Figure 8.13:
Concrete pads for timber trestle posts, dumped in a hedge behind English Nature's barn at Ridgemoreoak, 10 April 2004. *(M Shaw)*

Figure 8.14:
Hammer/Wire splicing tool (about 30cm. long) from the ropeway at the Bog Mine (it was part of the kit in a leather bag belonging to Mr Fountain). *(Shropshire Museums Service)*

1. SA (Shropshire Archives) DA/42/154/2 Chirbury RDC, roads correspondence and agreements with the mine company re the condition of road and the mine company's undertaking to carry out maintenance of their behalf. Shropshire lead Mines Ltd were willing to haul stone for road repairs from Snailbeach Sidings as a return load subject to financial agreement, the stone was to come by rail from Granham's Moor Quarry in that quarry's wagons.
2. Longueville Collection, SDR letter books National Library of Wales, courtesy of A Cuckson.
3. *The Snailbeach District Railways*, 1974. What was built was Railway Number 1, the originally proposed Railway Number 2 would have followed the contours round the two bigger valleys and involved some significant bridges, it was heading for Pennerley and the later proposed Shropshire Minerals Light Railway followed a similar proposed route but with major viaducts at the bigger dingles and would have gone to Gatten with a branch from Pennerley to Roman Gravels.
4. Information from "On the High Road, a history of Little Minsterley", P. Francis, 2001.
5. SA 4929/3/2
6. "Never on a Sunday", Shropshire Mines Trust, 2000.
7. SA SC3/1A1/7
8. As yet unpublished information provided by Mr R A Cooke.
9. Quoted in notes prepared for the AGM of the Railway and Canal Historical Association for their meeting in Shrewsbury in 1992, no source is given.
10. SA SC3/1A1/9
11. The 'Santander' information is from K.Lock and the rope removal item from the owner of the field behind Stiperstones School whose father tried to blow up the pylon base.
12. "A View from the Hills", states that the tramway came from a washing plant below the site of the former Miners Arms, this may have applied at some period but the route of the tramway from Ramsden's shaft appears to have gone towards the ropeway terminus rather than to a site by the former pub.
13. The Royal Engineers Journal, Volumes 35-36 Institution of Royal Engineers, 1922.
14. "A View from the Hills".
15. Mollie Rowson, "Never on a Sunday".
16. Henry Jones, "Never on a Sunday".
17. Electrical Journal, Volume 86, Dec 31st 1921, Pg 36 and The Royal Engineers Journal, op. cit.

9. Huglith Line

The ropeway from Bog was clearly successful enough to encourage Shropshire Mines Ltd. to further invest in the technology, presumably again from Ropeway Ltd. Huglith mine had been opened for barytes by the Wotherton Barytes and Lead Mining Company Ltd. about 1910, on a site which had in the nineteenth century provided a little copper. The mine passed on amalgamation in 1916 to Shropshire Mines Ltd. and to Malehurst Barytes Company Ltd. in 1925. It become part of Laporte's empire in 1932, though trading as Malehurst Barytes until the mine closed.

By the end of mining at Huglith in 1945 two other mines transported their produce there by lorry, for onward transmission by the ropeway. Gatten mine had started in the late eighteenth century looking for lead and copper, but it does not appear to have been a success. Barytes mining began late in the nineteenth century and the mine ended up with the Malehurst Barytes Co. via Shropshire Mines Ltd., by this time often being known as Brownhill mine. The Sallies mine was the last mine developed in this part of the county, in the late 1930s, though little seems to have happened until the mid 1940s. The Malehurst company hoped that this mine assisted by Gatten would keep Malehurst Mill supplied with barytes once Huglith mine was worked out. This was not to be and all three mines and the mill (at least for processing barytes) ceased functioning by 1948.

Huglith's barytes was initially trammed to the road where the present site entrance is and transferred to four-horse drays for the trip to Pontesbury Station, this carried on until the early 1920s (locally, convincingly said to be 1922) when the ropeway was built.

The County Council Roads and Bridges Committee agreed a ropeway crossing of the main road on 23rd July 1921 which must be the line from Huglith.[1] No more dates can be quoted until the liquidation of Shropshire Mines Ltd. when that agreement was finally transferred to Malehurst Barytes Co., on 12th Feb 1927 after the approval of the committee just over a year earlier.[2] The line then presumably ran smoothly until the closure of Huglith Mine in October 1945. That event did not however end the ropeway's life as barytes was taken by lorry from Gatten (Brownhill) and The Sallies mines for transfer to it. This finished with the closure of Gatten mine in November 1948 a month after The Sallies had succumbed. Most of the ropeway (and Huglith mine) was dismantled shortly after by Wappy Phillips the noted local scrap man. The last bit to go was the bridge over the main road at Poulton which Malehurst Barytes Co. themselves demolished starting at 5 o'clock one Sunday morning in 1950 or 1951. The workmen were threatened, by Bill Morgan, Malehurst site manager, to be on time or be sacked and they arrived on time, but the village policeman, needed to control the traffic, was late.[3]

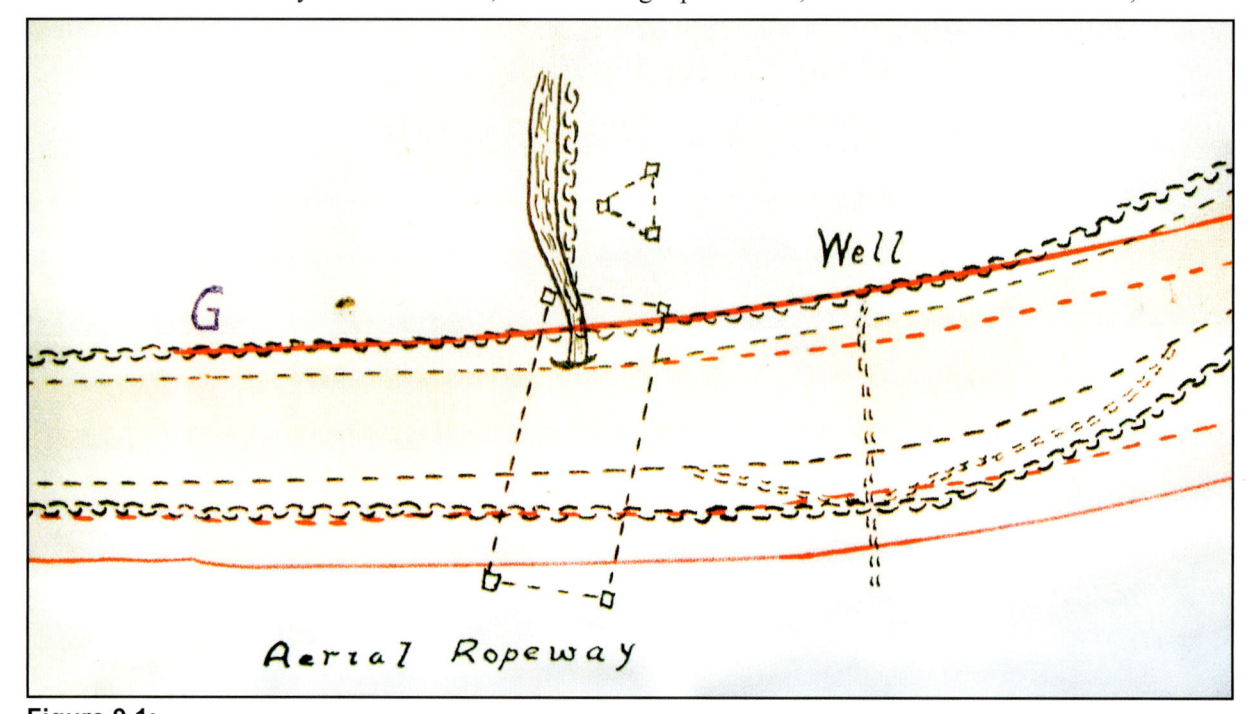

Figure 9.1:
Plan for the straightening of the main road at Poulton showing the Huglith ropeway crossing and a triangular trestle base. *(Shropshire Archives, R&B agreements 182, July 1926)*

Figure 9.2 (above):
Huglith ropeway loading station, in 1922.

Note: The first trestle is visible in the background and the bridge with the rope passing under it to the drive pit is in the foreground.

(K.C.Lock)

Figure 9.3:
A wooden trestle on the Huglith ropeway, believed to be near Malehurst Mill, (c1920) with bucket number 44 passing overhead.

(K.C.Lock)

SCMC Account 28 - Aerial Ropeways of Shropshire

Figure 9.4:
The ropeway terminus at Malehurst Mill in the 1920s.

The picture may have been taken during the construction of the mill c1925.

(Emily Griffiths Collection)

Unlike the Bog line, the Huglith ropeway was straight for its three and a half miles. It began with a sheave in a pit to the south of the track to the mine where presumably tensioning took place. The rope then passed under a bridge which carried that track and up through the loading bank to the first trestle. As at Bog most of the trestles were wooden with steel ones in places, the reasons for some of which are now lost. Few photographs are known to exist, but one (figure 9.5) shows what seems to be all wooden trestles most of the way from the mine to Poles Coppice. Just south of and in that coppice are three bases of triangular steel trestles (figure 11.13, page 61). It is not known whether these were always steel or if they were later replacement of wooden ones which could have been 20 or more years old.

The line crossed the Snailbeach railway and then the main road some yards to the east of the Bog line and arrived at Malehurst. The buckets were numbered on their sides with large white numerals, 44 is the highest noted and seven the only other one!(see figure 9.3). Little evidence remains to show how the loading bank worked. It was served by a tramway from the mine adit and after Huglith's closure by lorries. The ore was tipped into bins which in turn discharged bucket load by bucket load onto the ropeway (figure 9.2).

The only surviving wooden trestle base looks to be slightly different from those on the Bog line but as it is tipped in the hedge a field away from its original alignment it is impossible to be precise. The steel ones known of were, as stated above triangular and constructed of angle iron and round bar as shown in the only photograph of one. The bridge at Poulton was of steel with a triangular trestle to its south.[4] The terminus at Malehurst is illustrated and seems to have gone round the sides of a concrete bunker before discharging its load onto the hoist (figure 9.4). It appears not to have been automated as even in the late 1930s Cecil Mansell was employed to tip the buckets out as they arrived. The rope was probably very similar to Bog's and presumably the sheave at Malehurst was altered to carry the second rope when the Huglith line was built. Very little ever passed up the rope to the mine.

The telephone was used to alternate between ropeways with, in later years the Huglith line being run as needed in mid morning and mid afternoon, probably continuing a pattern established when both lines were working. Both ropeway probably ran at 5 miles per hour, this seems to have been fairly standard.

Less remains of the Huglith line than of the Bog one, with just the wheel pit at the mine, the three steel trestle bases at Poles coppice and a set of wooden bases in the hedge mentioned earlier, locations are given in the data list.

The mine produced almost 300,000 tonnes of barytes over its lifetime, most of this after the construction of the ropeway. Annual figures between 10 and 15,000 tonnes were normal which taking a 300 day working year give 130 to 200 bucket loads per day.

Figure 9.5:
A line of ropeway trestles 'marching' across the countryside from Huglith towards Poles Coppice.
(Authors Collection)

MINERS ON MILK DIET

How Daily Ration Reaches Huglith

The photograph illustrates the inauguration of a milk service at the works of the Malehurst Barytes Company at Minsterley. The Company operates the Huglith Mine from which the bartyes is conveyed by an overhead wire transporter to the malehurst Works, to be ground up into the product used as an ingredient of paint.

The same transporter is the means of conveying a supply of milk daily to the miners at Huglith. A mid-morning ration of milk is becoming an increasingly regular feature in factories, collieries and other industrial works throughout the country as a result of the campaign of the National Milk Publicity Council.

More than 6,000 industrial undertakings now have a milk service in operation for the benefit of their employees and the number of men and women making regualr use of these services is in the neighbourhood of half a million.

Workmen at Malehurst Barytes Mill enjoy their morning milk ration. The case of bottles is about to be sent up by overhead transporter to the men in the mine three miles away.

Figure 9.6:
In 1938 the Huglith line featured in the local press as part of a National Milk campaign.
(Shrewsbury Chronicle 5th feb. 1938)

---

1 SA (Shropshire Archives) SC3/1A1/9 Roads and Bridges Committee minutes
2 As above and SC/1/1B/1
3 Information from Esmond Betton whose Father, Harold worked on the demolition, Esmond was in Greece on National Service hence his uncertainty about the year.
4 Shown on a road widening plan of 1926, SA SCC records R&B agreements 182, this was to straighten a bend, the ropeway bridge was over the very edge of the affected area but did not need any alteration.

10. Ropeway Staff

Not much is known of the men who worked these lines.

A man, probably called Gilderson surveyed and set out the Bog route and perhaps supervised the traction engines bringing the rope and pylon components from the station, no doubt Minsterley. Edward Fountain 'came and took over'[1] and spliced the ropes, a job previously done we are told by Mr Bunting (of Bunting Shaft fame at the Bog mine).

For a time a Jim Williams oiled the wheels on the Bog line most Mondays.[2] Later the Huglith line's wheels were done, apparently fortnightly, by Tom Heath from Bentlawnt who used to start at Malehurst and walk to Huglith with a tub of grease on his back, climbing every pylon. As soon as he reached Huglith, he would turn round and walk back to Malehurst.[3] Paul Measler, a German school teacher, caught here on holiday at the beginning of the World War II, is remembered as having worked on the line. The POWs used to make and sell craftwork, e.g. picture frames and rings, to supplement their diet. They seemed to have been treated in a fairly relaxed manner. George Betton, the grandfather of the late Esmond Betton (who himself worked on the ropeway), was the sergeant of the platoon who guarded them. Specific manning for the Bog ropeway seems to have been three men and three boys, two men at Bog, one of each at Malehurst and two boys (presumable not at the same time or no work would have got done?) at Beach Hill.

The late Esmond Betton has provided much useful information, he worked (and lived) at Huglith as a young man. His involvement with the ropeway was the filling of buckets (or breaking up the contents of the ore bins in frosty weather so that the buckets could be filled). He assisted on the line until its final closure. After the mine at Huglith closed just three men were left there to work the ropeway, Will Evans helped by Ned Davies and Esmond Betton.

The story is told of the man who used to ride home in a bucket from the Bog and jump out at the cutting on Beach Hill, one night, perhaps after yet another runaway he dreamt that he did not get out on time, he did not travel again. Another story is told of the man who rode the Huglith line for a wager from Malehurst to its lowest point near Huglith Farm where he jumped out. Both these stories are convincing, but would be more so if the protagonist in each case had not just been remembered as 'Williams'. Other men are said, no doubt correctly to have travelled in buckets and in one case had to choose between staying up all night or jumping out after the line unexpectedly stopped.

Figure 10.1:
Mr. Esmond Betton (right) explaining the operation of the Huglith ropeway terminus to Michael Shaw (left) during a visit to Huglith mine, April 2005.
(K Lake - I A Recordings)

---

1 'A View from the hills'
2 Mollie Rowson remembered seeing him at the Stiperstones School trestle, from 'Never on a Sunday'
3 Pers. com. Esmond Betton

11. Fieldwork

Bog Line Fieldwork

A group numbering between one and nine[1] met on Tuesdays evenings in the early Summer of 2003 to plot the remains of the Bog ropeway and its branches. As soon as we arrived at the transfer station on the first evening everyone began delving, sighting, measuring, photographing, videoing, recording etc. After seven evenings the locations of the loading point at Bog, the transfer station above Burgam Mine, ten other trestle bases of the main run and two on the branch to Buxton Quarry had been identified running from Bog to a point north west of Snailbeach village. The bases at Bog, the transfer station, behind the school and beyond Snailbeach are for steel trestles the remainder for wooden ones. Some remains are ex-situ, in one case well off the line of the ropeway.

The search for trestle bases carried on north of Snailbeach on succeeding Tuesday evenings The country is rather more intensively farmed and hopes were not as high as previously, but we need not have worried. The bases found pushed into the dingle just to the south of the Plox Green Snailbeach road (Fig. 11.2) were revisited in better light and it proved to contain thirteen, seven for timber posts and the remainder for a steel trestle and (presumably) its struts. At this stage the line of the ropeway was still unclear and as none of these bases were in their original position their evidence was doubtful. Ultimately we decided that the steel trestle bases were more or less on the line and had formed an angle station where the route changed by about twelve degrees and headed for Malehurst.

A 1921 article in The Electrical Journal found a decade after this survey and referred to elsewhere stated that the line curved over seven pylons and that the actual change of direction was just under seven degrees. The seven timber post foundations no doubt did not come from far away.

A further set of 'steel' bases was found in another dingle, again proving to be not far from their original position. Inspection then moved to Minsterley football field. A set of 'timber' bases was found just to the north, 2 in the hedge and 2 in situ. A further short distance north and a set of four timber bases was found in the hedge where Callow Lane was crossed. A local history book revealed that there was a set of bases straddling the rear boundary of number 7, Little Minsterley[2]. This was initially unlocatable due to the crop in the field but on the last evening's visit, after harvest it was found. The relevant parts of the site at Malehurst are somewhat overgrown and need a winter visit. The final act was to measure up the terminus at Bog Mine immediately following the completion of which some of the assembled multitude were summoned to a rescue at Otter Hole.

Figure 11.1:
Two bases for the legs of a timber trestle in a field near Snailbeach football ground (B44 on Map1).
(K Lake - I A Recordings)

Figure 11.2:
One of the bases for the leg of a steel trestle discovered amongst others in a dingle near the Plox Green - Snailbeach road (B48b on Map 1).
(K Lake - I A Recordings)

---

1 Pedants may have difficulties with 'a group of one', so what…
2 Information from 'On the High Road'

SCMC Account 28 - Aerial Ropeways of Shropshire

There have very clearly been many more bases than we have found, some, as at the reservoir and in the one dingle have been grubbed out and moved, others may still remain to be found but apart from Malehurst and Perkins Beach little seems to be gained by further searching. Assuming trestles in cultivated parts to be at around 100m centres there may have been between 60 and 75 of them. George Evans' book says that he thinks that there were 127 buckets in all. These figures suggest that there were perhaps 60 trestles each with one bucket between them and a few buckets over as all would never be on the line at one time. This suggested spacing is supported by a lease for the land at Hogstow which specifies that there were to be no more than eight trestles of timber or steel The accompanying plan (it is not clear whether it was a survey or a proposal; as it was prepared almost a year after the lease became valid it) shows seven (see figure 8.4, page 40), with the distance between trestles between 100 and 200 yards (or a slightly smaller number of metres).

In 2014, one of the Tuesday evening walks was given over to re-examining the route of the Bog ropeway, during which more accurate GPS locations for various bases were obtained. In addition a previously undiscovered steel trestle base was found in-situ.

Figure 11.3:
SCMC members making trial excavations to locate the ropeway terminus at the Bog.
(K Lake - I A Recordings)

Figure 11.4:
David Poyner measuring base 'd' (see Fig.11.7) at the Bog terminus. *(I.A.Cooper)*

Figure 11.5:
SCMC members making trial excavations to locate the ropeway terminus at the Bog - using an old photograph (Fig. 8.8) to calculate the positions of the bolts - with amazing success!.
(K Lake - I A Recordings)

Figure 11.6:
SCMC members measuring wall 'e' (see Fig.11.7) of the Bog terminus. *(I.A.Cooper)*

The Bog Mine Aerial Ropeway Terminus

Over June-August of 2014, the Club were given permision to examine the terminus of the aerial ropeway at the Bog mine (SO360 979). This concluded with exploratory excavations, to try and clarify how the ropeway worked.

The Bog mine was one of the earliest and most important lead mines in the area. However, in the early 20th century, when it was operated by Shropshire Lead Mines Ltd/Shropshire Mines Ltd, production had switched from lead to barytes. This period saw considerable investment at the Bog, most notably the sinking of Ramsden's shaft to open new ground to the south of the old workings. The mine had always relied on road transport to take its products away; a link with the Snailbeach District Railways would have involved crossing steep and difficult terrain. However, in 1917/18 a new mode of transport was adopted by the construction of an aerial ropeway from the mine to a site adjoining the Minsterley branch of the Great Western/London and North Western joint line at Malehurst. This worked until the closure of the Bog Mine in 1925. Most of the site was cleared, but the concrete bases of the ropeway terminus remained visible until the 1970s, after which they were buried during further clearance work. Today all that is visible on the surface is a shallow cutting on an approximate north-south alignment, representing the final few yards of the ropeway before it entered the terminus and a row of machine bases south-east of these.

The most obvious features on the site today are three machine bases (a, b and c in figure 11.7). These are aligned parallel to the ropeway cutting and are all made of concrete set on brick bases. Beyond base (a) there are the remains of a brick wall (d in figure 11.7); there is evidence of a return at its eastern end. A number of concrete rectangular bases with associated holding down bolts (e, f, g and h, figure 11.7) can be found just below the surface, in line with the shallow cutting. All of these were visible on the photograph (figure 8.9, p.44) of the site prior to infilling and (e) and (h) were investigated by excavation using a mini-digger.

Only the positions of the holding down bolts for bases (f) and (g) were recorded. Base (e) was 16' long by 1'4" wide. The central 5' were raised by a few inches and held the two holding bolts at 4' centre. The base extended 4'2" below the surface on a slight batter to a concrete floor present at either end. This was not present

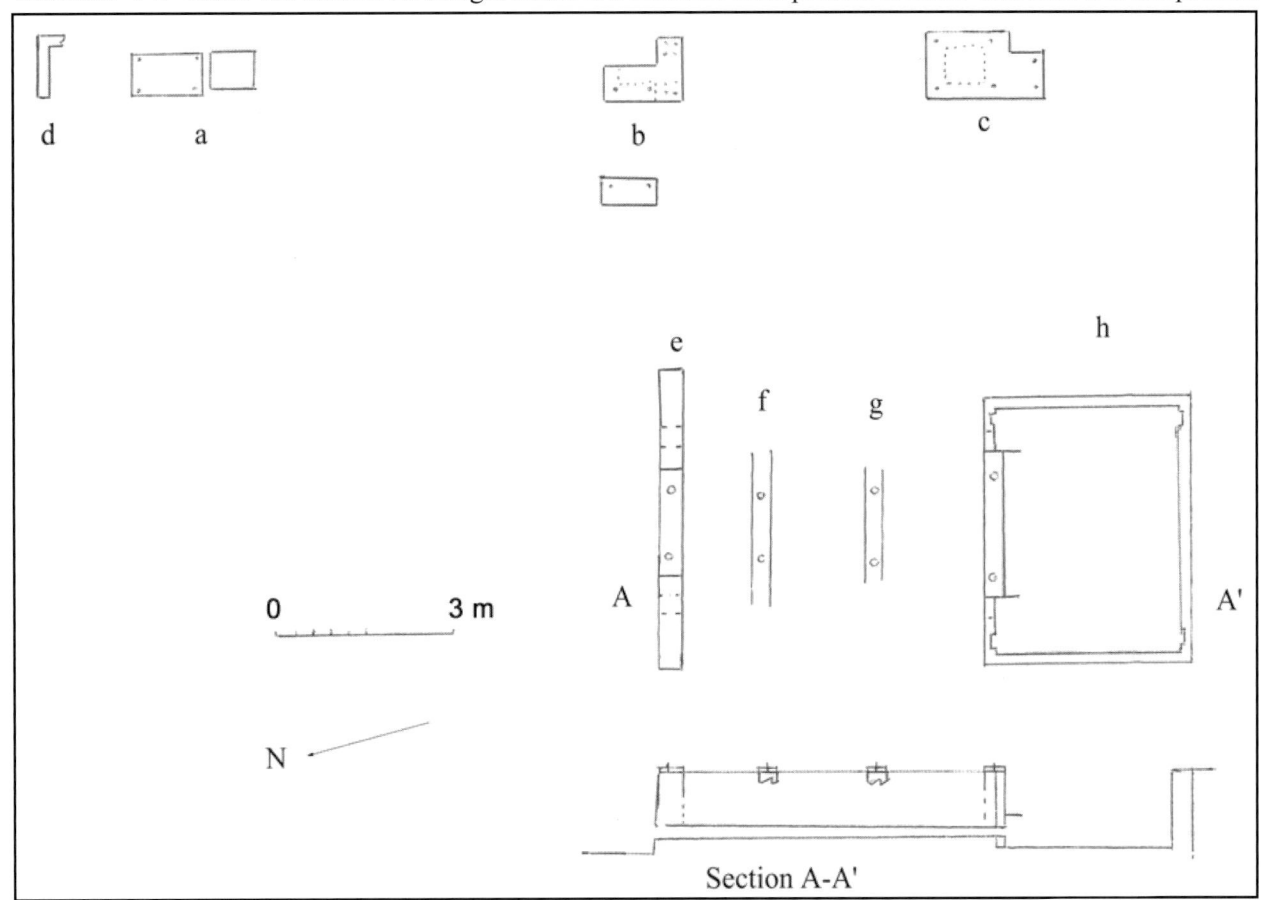

Figure 11.7:
 Bases at the remains of the ropeway terminus. The main figure shows these in plan form. In the bottom right hand corner there is a section showing the relationship of the rope culverts to the drive pit.

Figure 11.8:
A photograph of the Bog ropeway terminus from before 1922, with the concrete bases (e, f, g, and h) excavated by the club in 2014 highlighted. *(The Electrical Journal, Volume 86, Dec 31st 1921, Pg 36)*

in the centre of the structure, at least at this depth, although recording was difficult as the water table was above the height of the trench. One yard from either end of the wall were two holes cut into the concrete; each was 3' from the top of the wall and they were 12" long by 7" deep.

Feature (h) is a concrete pit; the wall goes down 4' to a concrete floor. A 14" x 8"hole was found at the same depth and exactly aligned with the corresponding hole in the west end of wall (e); there can be little doubt that they form a culvert. It is presumed that a corresponding culvert exists to connect the other hole in wall (e) with the pit. Whilst the pit was 4' deep by the hole, next to the holding down bolts there was a concrete plinth. It was not possible to measure this, but it seems likely that here the pit is only around 2'6" deep. Some 100 feet from wall (e) were two bolts set 13" apart, set in the base of a (stone?) building, 6' wide by 9' long. These bolts aligned with the eastern holding down bolts on walls e-g and pit h.

The interpretation of the site has been facilitated by the discovery of an article in the Electrical Journal (Volume 86, Dec 31st 1921) which contains a description of the ropeway and a photograph of the terminus (see above). Apart from the photograph, the article reveals that at the tension in the rope was provided by a 4 ton weight, which, working via a 4:1 system, provided a force of 16 tons.

The supports for the ropeway are clear in the photograph and correspond to bases (e), (f) and (g). These carried iron frames to carry the rope to (h), which is seen to be the driving pit with two large vertical wheels. A schematic interpretation of the driving and tension arrangements is shown in figure 11.10. In the photograph (figure 11.8), the vertical wheel nearest the camera (wheel a' in figure 11.10) has teeth cut in its outside edge, indicating that it engaged with a smaller spur wheel hidden in the bottom of the pit. Somehow, this spur wheel must have been connected to the electric motor; as it rotated, it provided the drive to turn the larger wheel and hence move the rope. The further vertical wheel (a in figure 11.10) may also have been driven but it is impossible to tell from the photograph and it may simply have rotated freely on its axle; it would have had to move in the opposite direction to the nearside wheel. Both of these wheels must have been around 6' in diameter, based on the dimensions of the pit.

The rope passed around the vertical wheel, through the one culvert in the concrete and out through the hole in wall (figure 11.8, e). Here it passed round a return wheel (b in figure 11.10), to go back through the other culvert, round the second vertical wheel and so back onto the pylons. The return wheel would have been around 9' in diameter, to match the width between the culverts.

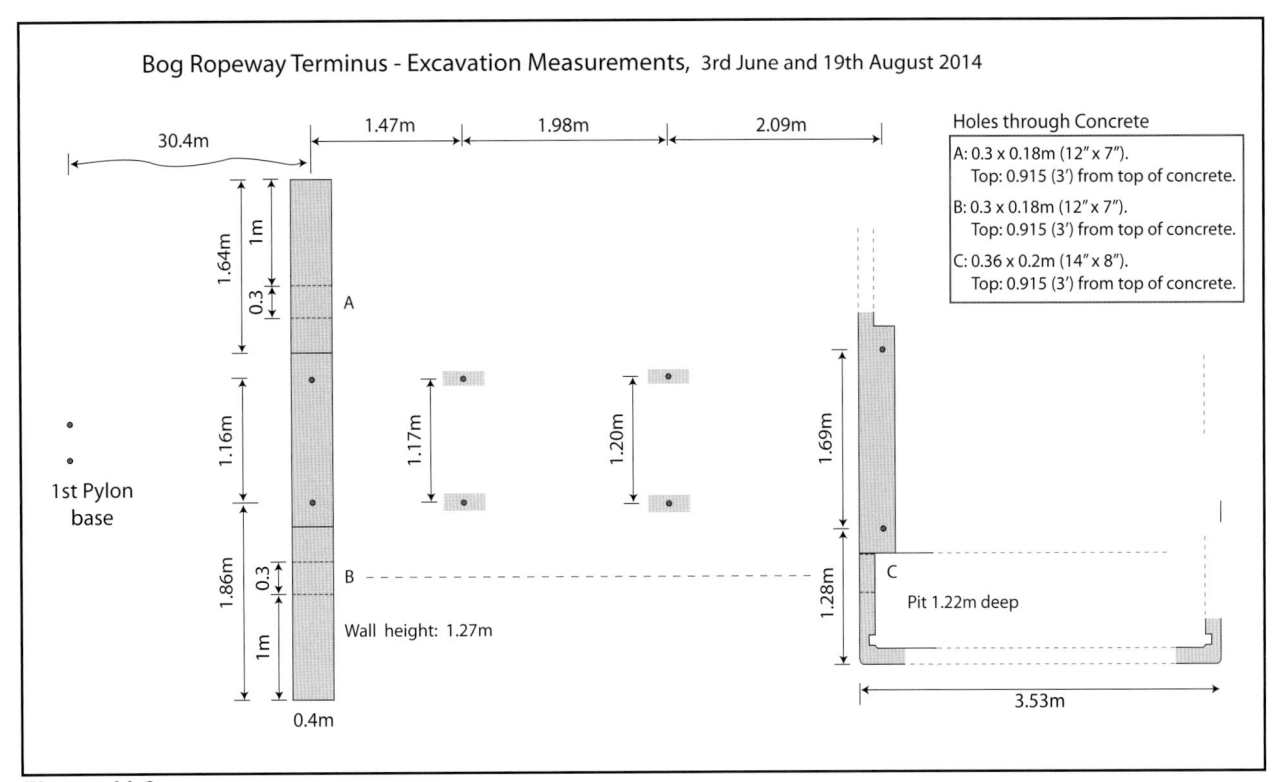

Figure 11.9:
Detail measurements of the bases at the remains of the Bog ropeway terminus excavated in 2014 by the Shropshire Caving and Mining Club.

Rope Stretch

In the course of operation, the wire rope would stretch; the 11 mile rope needed to go to Malehurst and back again might easily be expected to stretch by 100 feet over the course of its working life. Consequently, it would be necessary to allow the return wheel to move, to take up this stretch. If this did not happen, the rope would become slack and would slip on the driving wheel. The typical arrangement was to mount the return wheel on a trolley so it could be moved back and forwards on rails or skids. Little physical evidence was uncovered during the survey and excavation as to how this worked and so the arrangement shown in figure 11.10 is based on analogy with other systems, such as the working example at Claughton, Lancashire (which used skids).

It is suggested that there were rails set on the concrete floors at the base of wall (figure 11.8, e), which may have extended through the cutting for around 100 feet. The trolley (figure 11.10, d) with the return wheel would have been mounted on these rails and connected at its one end via a 4:1 pulley system (f) to the 4 ton weight (g) mentioned in the description of the ropeway. To tension the main rope it is surmised that the winch (figure 11.10, e) was used to lift the 4 ton weight to the top of it's 'headframe'. The winch was then locked off and the trolley (d) 'released' and the weight allowed to descend pulling the trolley to tighten the main rope. Once tight the trolley was 'locked-off' and the winch used to lower the heavy weight, so it rested on the floor and so taking the strain off the tensioning system.

It is possible that the pair of bolts 100 feet from the wall (figure 11.8, e) may have been connected with this presumed tensioning system, if they were not the base of a normal trestle. The foundations in which these bolts sit is curious; no building in this position is shown on the 1902 OS map of the mine, but it is difficult to see why such a structure would have been made for the ropeway.

The drive to the ropeway and the functions of the machine bases remain matters for speculation. To achieve a maximum rope speed of 120 yards/minute, the driving wheel would need to rotate at 18 rpm. Given that the motor ran at 726 rpm, there would need to be a 40:1 reduction; if this was done in a single step, the spur wheel that engaged with the drive wheel would need to be 1.8" in diameter! Thus there must have been at least one intermediate gear wheel and shaft. It is most likely that the motor driving the ropeway was located in the brick building in figure 11.8; it's base (possibly c on figure 11.7) inside the building might have held the motor and a drive shaft going to the pit. There is no sign in figure 11.8 of any shafting between the brick building and the drive pit but it is possible that this cannot be seen due to the angle of the photograph. Base b (figure 11.8) must have been in the corrugated iron building attached to the north wall of the building. The way it and base (c) are aligned with the presumed motor suggest all three were connected in some way, but their function(s) are unclear.

A full report of the project was made for Shropshire Council and the Bog Centre and a copy is available on the Club website (see www.shropshirecmc.org.uk/reports/bog-ropeway1.pdf).

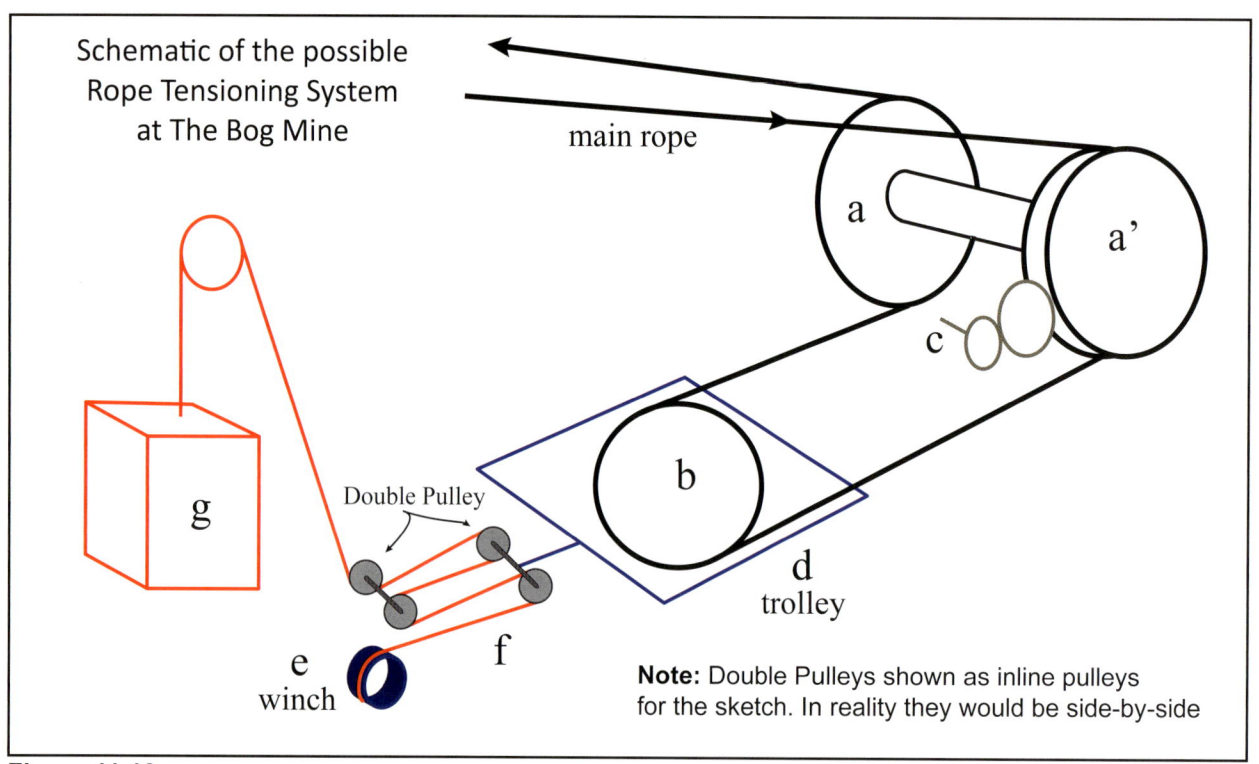

Figure 11.10:
Schematic drawing showing a possible reconstruction of the main features of the site. **a**, **a'**, driving wheels for the rope; **b**, return wheel; **c** hypothetical drive from the motor to the driving wheel; **d**, trolley on rails (not shown) allowing the return wheel to be moved backwards to tension the system. Winch; **e**, used to 'lift' the 4 ton weight, **g**, to the top of its 'headframe' (not shown), via **f**, the hypothetical 4:1 block and pulley system.

Figure 11.11:
An old tensioning trolley on the Claughton ropeway, Lancashire. It is probably similar to that utilised at the Bog. The large pulley on the left is the main return sheave wheel for the ropeway, while the smaller wheel is part of the tensioning system.
(Claughton Ropeway)

Huglith Line Fieldwork

A similar band of souls met on Tuesday evenings in 2004 to look for remains of the Huglith ropeway. At the mine a square pit which must have been more or less in line with the ropeway was noted, previously it had been considered to have been a small shaft. The mystery was later resolved (April 2005) when we met Esmond Betton on site who confirmed that it was the pit for the return sheave of the ropeway, thus providing a clear alignment.

The land on this route provides much better farming and many more bases have been totally lost. A couple of sets were found dumped in a dingle, though the farmer remembered digging them out and was able to indicate their one-time locations (see Hx, H14 & H15 on Map 2, page 67). The only place where a worthwhile amount was found was around Poles Coppice where three sets of bases (H31, H32 and H33 on Map 2) were found.

Figure 11.12:
Pit for the Huglith ropeway return sheave.
(K Lake - I A Recordings)

Figure 11.13:
Remains of a steel trestle base in Poles Coppice.
(M Shaw)

Perkins Beach Line Fieldwork

A walk over Beach Hill at Christmas 2014 revealed a trestle base buried in the heather, after one of the party stepped into the hole in the middle of one of the blocks! Also on the track up Perkins Beach a concrete area was discovered that appeared to line-up not only with the base on the brow of the hill but also the Transfer station. It is thought to be the site for the portable engine that worked the ropeway.

A conversation with local resident Joan Purslow, confirmed that this was the site of the ropeway terminus, having been told so by her father.

Fig 11.14 (left):
Discovery of the overgrown base on Beach Hill (see PB on Map 1 & Map 3).
(I.A.Cooper)

Fig 11.15 (right):
Possible terminus of the Perkins Beach ropeway. The concrete pad (marked with arrow) aligns with the base and transfer station on top of the hill - illustrated by the telegraph pole.
(I.A.Cooper)

12. Imaginary ropeways

At various time for various reasons ropeways that do not exist have appeared in print so it seems sense to draw attention to these so as to try and avoid confusion. Two of them occur as a result of Eric Tonks' book "The Snailbeach District Railways". On the map of the railway in the 1974 edition a ropeway is marked which appears to go from Callow Hill to Malehurst but it is quite clear from the text that he knew that this was not so.[1] However a Callow Hill ropeway has appeared in print since no, doubt on the strength of Tonks.

Also mentioned in Tonks (though only the 1950 edition), and much less explicable is the suggestion of a ropeway from 'Gravels mine' to Snailbeach smelter, this raises its head from time to time, including a query during the writing of this piece.

Confusion has been caused by the suggestion of a ropeway from Potter's Pit to Pennerley mine between 1882 and 1884. Though at that date some sort of ropeway could have been rigged up, the system had not fully developed. What did go between the two mines was a rope which wound Potter's Pit's shaft using Pennerley's engine. This line ran on upright pylons or 'rolleys', it is not difficult to see a possible confusion.

The last in this category is truly scary and totally imaginary. Malcolm Saville in the late 1940s wrote children's adventure stories set around the Stiperstones and in 'Seven White Gates' of 1944 some of his heroes inter-alia travel on a ropeway which features on the book's cover. It was drawn, no doubt in good faith, by someone who has had a ropeway described but never seen one. It is, thankfully unlike any actual ropeway, consisting of a large kibble with step irons to ride on and an external brake. Having four ropes vertically and possibly no intermediate pylons it seems to have been more like a Blondin than a true ropeway. The concept of a chute from the end of the ropeway to the valley bottom could be quite a novel concept in ore breaking. The cover pictures of various editions of 'Seven White Gates' showing different 'buckets' are reproduced here.

A nice aside to this tall tale is that I was made aware of the book by Tom Wall then of English Nature and his new barn HQ on the track from above Bog to Tankerville has a set of bases for a wooden trestle within its curtilage.

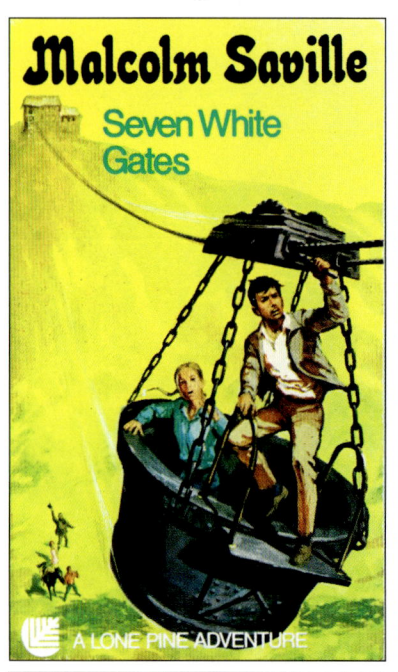

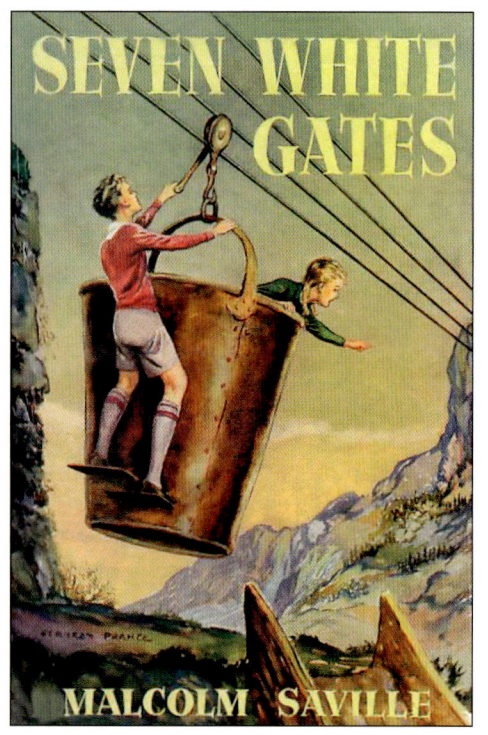

Figure 12.1: Various dust covers of "Seven White Gates" by Malcolm Saville.

above) Cover of the first edition. Published September 1944 by Newnes. Illustrations by Bertram Prance.

far left) Cover of the paperback 1970 Armada edition. Reprinted 1974/5.

left) Cover of the 1962 Dutch edition in the 'Prisma Juniores' series by "Het Spectrum". The ropeway tub looks more like a mine tub on this cover.

---

1 The 1950 edition map is sufficiently different that it is clear that the ropeway comes from beyond Callow Hill Quarry

13. Bibliography & Acknowledgements

Books referred to, not otherwise referenced in the text:

Francis P, et al, *Never on a Sunday,* Shropshire Mines Trust, 2000
Tonks E, *The Snailbeach District Railways,* Industrial Railway Society, 1950 and 1974
Francis P, *On the High Road, a history of Little Minsterley*, P Francis, 2001
Evans George, *A Voice from the Hills,* Muriel Regde, Minsterley, 2003
Industrial Railway Record, The journal of the Industrial Railway Society published by them.
Saville Malcolm, *Seven White Gates*, George Newnes, London, 1944

Acknowledgements

We would like to thank various people for their assistance not least the members of the Shropshire Caving & Mining Club who spent a series of Tuesday evenings searching for, surveying and photographing ropeway remains on the Stiperstones, and various other sites around the County, without their assistance there would be a lot less information available.

Little did we know in 2003 when we started this project as the Club "Summer walks" programme, that we would still be finding new remains and information about the ropeways throughout Shropshire over a decade later!

Photographs and information are also acknowledged with thanks from the late Pat Barry, Keith Beddoes, the late Esmond Betton, the late Geoffrey Bramall, Anthony Brick, the late Neville Brick, Bing Cooper, the late Ben Crowther, John Derricutt, Eric Edwards, the custodians of the Emily Griffiths collection, Bob Handley, Robert Hodge, David Lloyd, the late Ken Lock, Roy Philpotts, George Poyner, Chris Woodward, the Alveley Historical Society and Shropshire Archives.

Plus several people from the area who remember the ropeways themselves or who remember others talking of them have added little bits of information here and there, sometimes on the roadside, or by telephone, or over a pint!

Figures 13.1 & 13.2:
Help has often come from unexpected quarters!

Inquisitive cattle, June 2003, helping us examine the bases by the footpath near Snailbeach Football Club.

Appendix A - Schedule of Bases found during Fieldwork

Bog Main line

The reference in the first column below refers to Map 1 on page 65. The 'numbers' have been allocated to the trestles, starting from the Bog terminus and assuming there was a trestle approximately every 100m. Should more bases be discovered, hopefully they will fit into the sequence. It must be stressed that this numbering sequence does not relate to original trestle numbers, unfortunately those details have yet to be discovered.

Map ref	N.G. Ref.	Details
BT		**Bog terminus.**
	SO 35580 97901	Main section of Bog terminus.
	SO 35581 97893	Most southerly bolt of the foundations at the Bog terminus.
	SO 35585 97907	Most northerly bolt of the foundations at the Bog terminus.
B01	SO 35585 97926	Possible site of the first trestle on the ropeway.
B02	SO 35610 98025	Single bolt by road by former Bog School. Probable remains of the 6 base trestle visible in an old postcard.
B07	SO 35768 98510	Gate with view of one large block in distance.
B12	SO 35893 99022	Four blocks.
B17	SO 36024 99497	Four blocks in gorse, 2.1m separation.
TX		**Transfer Station (connection to Perkins Beach & Buxton Quarry lines)**
B18	SO 36042 99613	Trestle base - one block by hedge, 13.5m from main base.
B19	SO 36062 99622	Site of transfer station main holding-down bolts.
B21	SO 36113 99809	Two blocks above cutting, one with deep hole.
B22	SO 36122 99841	Top of cutting.
B23	SO 36130 99870	Four Blocks below cutting.
B24	SJ 36259 00299	Three bolts behind Stiperstones school 4.5m separation, with a stay base in the next field.
B28	SJ 36306 00668	Single block by gate on track (ex-situ).
B41	SJ 36717 01924	Four blocks by hedge (one in the hedge), 2.8m separation, 25cm holes in the concrete bases.
B43	SJ 36782 02153	Set of four bases in-situ on brow of bank above stream.
B44	SJ 36813 02247	Two blocks in field, 2.8m separation. It is believed that the angle of the ropeway changed by 7° over the next 7 trestles from B44 past B48.
B48	SJ 36900 02639	Flattened area in field, possible former location of a base.
B48b	SJ 36919 02706	Five large concrete bases with a 1" BSW stud protruding from centre, dumped in a steep sided streamway, some have lengths of angle iron attached. Plus seven pads for wooden poles (overgrown).
B56	SJ 37264 03408	Three blocks by stream (ex-situ).
B71	SJ 37884 04815	Blocks in field, one in-situ, two in hedge.
B72	SJ 37919 04930	Four blocks by bush (one with a very large hole).
B75	SJ 38062 05253	Large block on edge of field, with bolt behind No.7 Little Minsterley.
MM	SJ 38408 05988	Approximate location of Malehurst terminus.

Map 1 - Route of the Bog Ropeway

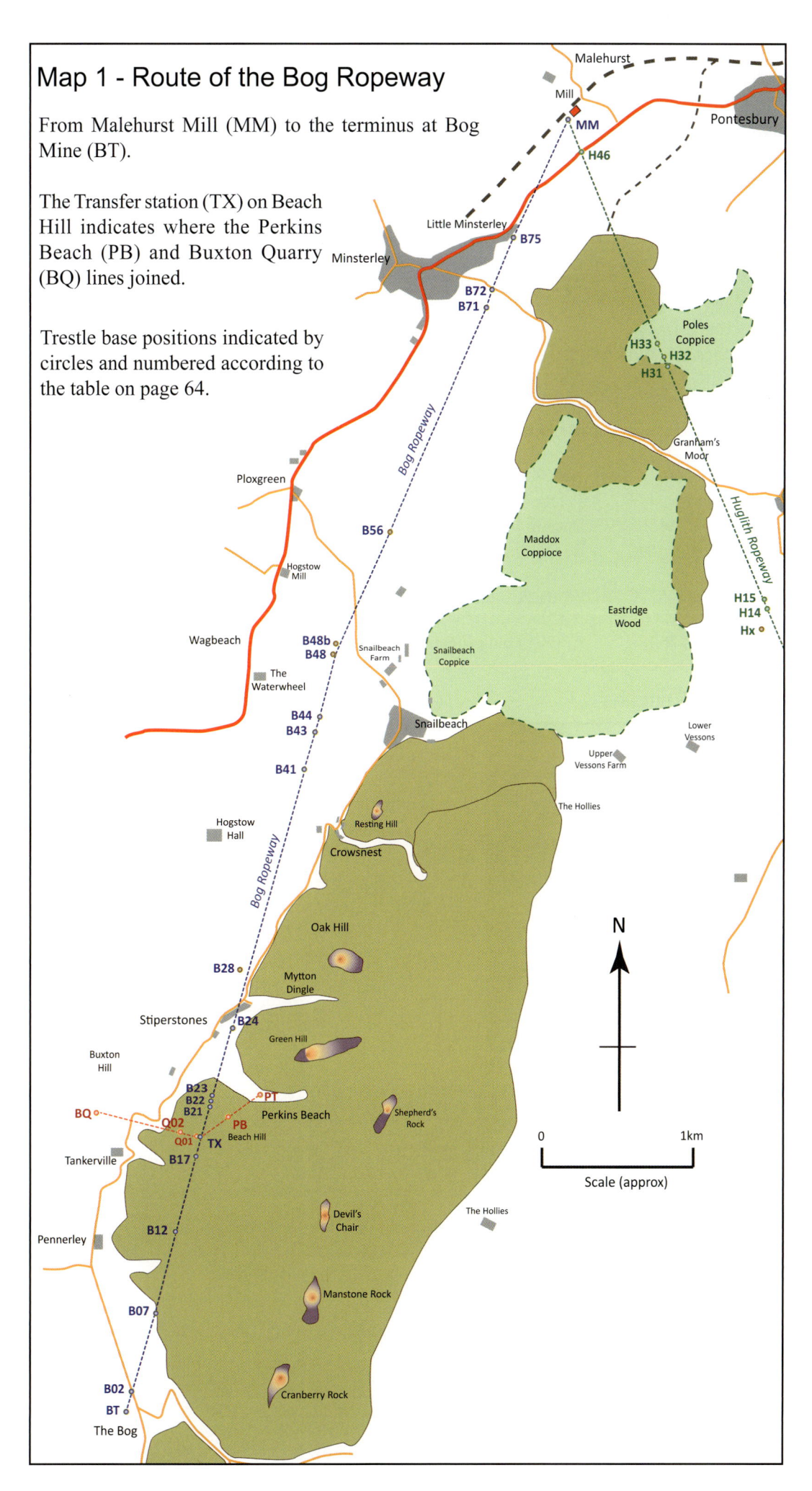

From Malehurst Mill (MM) to the terminus at Bog Mine (BT).

The Transfer station (TX) on Beach Hill indicates where the Perkins Beach (PB) and Buxton Quarry (BQ) lines joined.

Trestle base positions indicated by circles and numbered according to the table on page 64.

Huglith Line

A similar numbering system has been used for the trestle remains along the Huglith line as to that applied to the Bog line. It has been assumed, again, that there was a trestle approximately every 100m.

See Map 2 on page 67 for the line of the route from Malehurst Mill (MM) to the terminus at Huglith Mine (HT).

Map ref	N.G. Ref.	Details
HT		**Huglith terminus.**
	SJ 40315 01565	Pit which once held the return sheave wheel for the ropeway.
	SJ 40304 01590	Site of loading area.
H01	SJ 40285 01620	First trestle from loading area.
Hx	SJ 39678 02798	Pile of former base blocks in a hedge.
H14	SJ 39710 02923	Former site of trestle base (details from the farmer).
H15	SJ 39693 02984	Former site of trestle base (details from the farmer).
H31	SJ 39063 04443	Trestle base remains near Poles Coppice.
H32	SJ 39038 04505	Base in upper part of Poles Coppice.
H33	SJ 38995 04590	Base in lower part of Poles Coppice.
H46	SJ 38496 05777	Probable site of the Poulton road crossing.
MM	SJ 38408 05988	Approximate location of Malehurst terminus.

Huglith Ropeway Remains

Remains of the Huglith line have been hard to track down. Even those in Poles Coppice (**H32, left**) can be difficult to spot!

We were shown the large pile of bases (**Hx, below**) by the farmer on an exceedingly wet, gloomy summer evening in 2004. Making it extremely difficult to record the remains!

They appeared to be a mix of wood trestle and steel trestle bases.

Locations can be seen on Map 2.

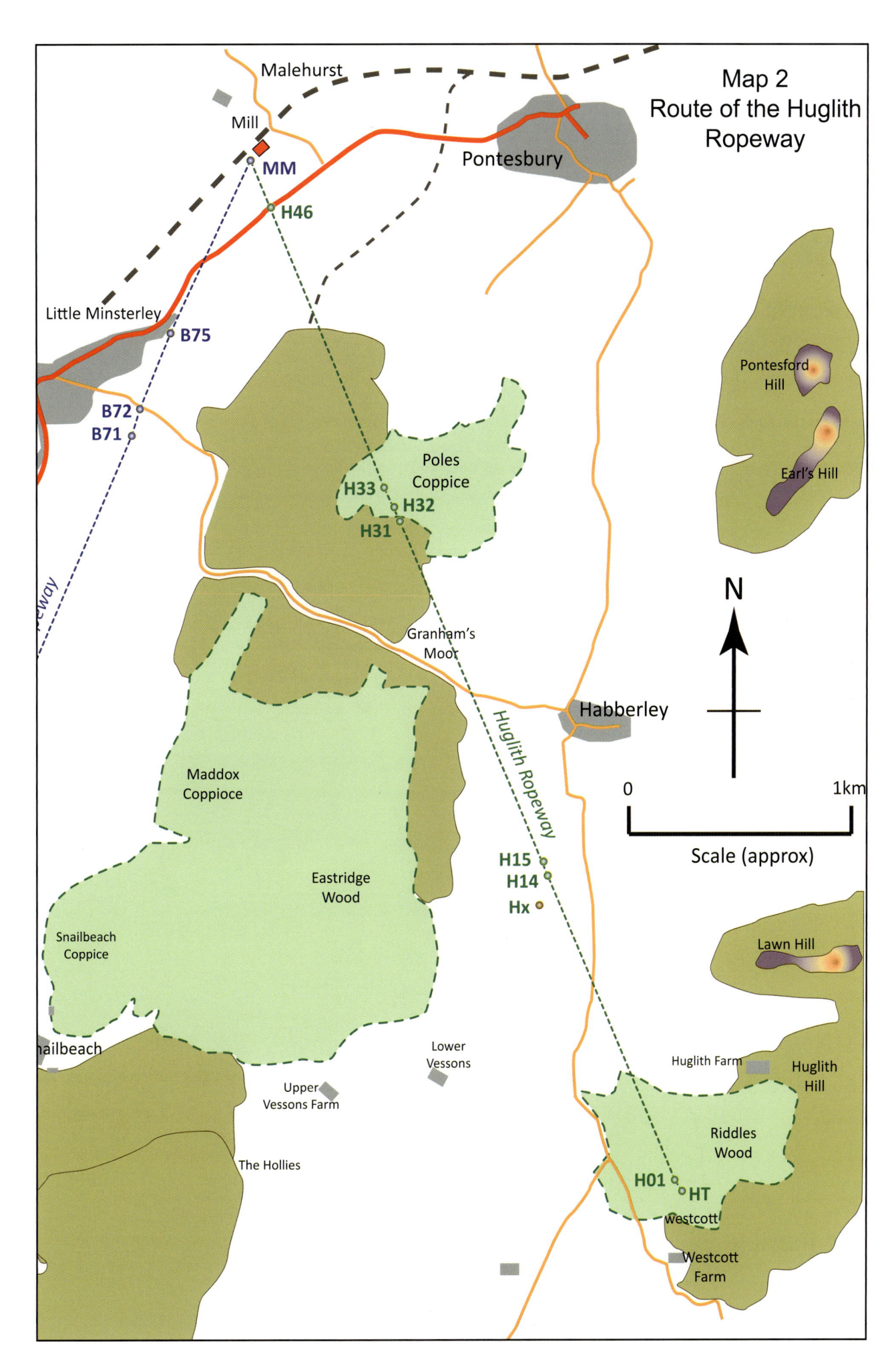

**Map 2
Route of the Huglith
Ropeway**

Perkins Beach Line

See Map 3 (below) for the line of the route from the Transfer station (TX) on the Main line to the possible terminus in Perkins Beach (PT).

Map ref	N.G. Ref.	Details
TX	SO 36062 99622	**Transfer Station (connection to Main line)**
PB	SO 36226 99739	Trestle base on Perkins Beach line on flank of Beach Hill.
PT	SO 36433 99889	Concrete pad, possibly the base for the portable engine at the Tabertail terminus of the Perkins Beach line.

Buxton Quarry Line

See Map 3 for the line of the route from the Transfer station (TX) on the Main line to the possible terminus in Buxton Quarry (BQ).

Map ref	N.G. Ref.	Details
TX	SO 36062 99622	**Transfer Station (connection to Main line)**
Q01	SO 36039 99620	Four transfer station blocks on the Buxton line - probably the first trestle.
Q02	SO 35927 99645	Three Blocks on the route down to Buxton quarry.
BQ	SO 35374 99764	Buxton quarry.

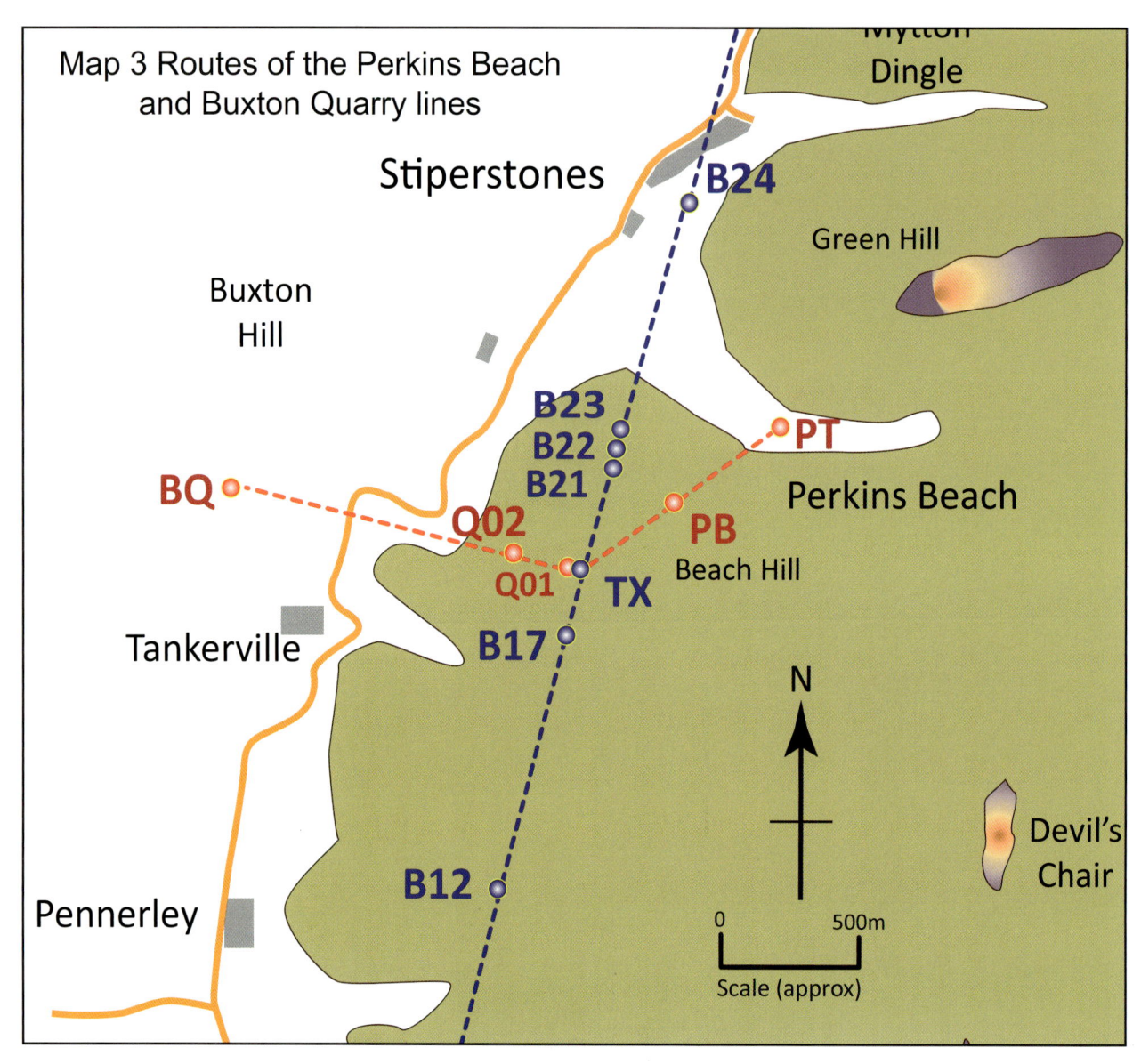

Map 3 Routes of the Perkins Beach and Buxton Quarry lines